RUSH
HOUR
MEALS

RECIPES FOR THE ENTIRE FAMILY

ROSE REISMAN

whitecap

EDITOR: Tracy Bordian
DESIGN: Diane Robertson
FOOD PHOTOGRAPHY: Mike McColl
FOOD STYLING: Patrick Engel
PROOFREADER: Joan Templeton

Library and Archives Canada Cataloguing in Publication

Reisman, Rose, 1953-, author
    Rose Reisman's rush hour meals.

ISBN 978-1-77050-303-8 (paperback)

    1. Quick and easy cooking. 2. Cookbooks.
I. Title.

TX833.5.R45 2016   641.5'55   C2016-900624-7

We acknowledge the financial support of the Government of Canada and the Province of British Columbia through the Book Publishing Tax Credit.

Nous reconnaissons l'appui financier du gouvernement du Canada et la province de la Colombie-Britannique par le Book Publishing Tax Credit.

Canada

21 20 19 18 17 16   1 2 3 4 5 6 7

Printed in Canada

DEDICATION

For my wonderful husband of close to 40 years, Sam, and for my darling children, Natalie, her husband Ricky, David, Laura, her fiancé Mark and Adam, who every day teach me about life and communication and how to be a supportive parent. And for the two newest members of my family: my daughter Natalie's twin baby girls, Chloe and Emma—my two granddaughters!

For the four animals with whom I share the quiet moments of my day: my two German Shepherds, Rocky and AJ, and my two cats, Misty and Ozzie.

A woman must have good friendships to balance her days. This book is also for my buddies, Kathy and Susan, who are always there for me.

CONTENTS

PREFACE

LIFE JUST SEEMS TO BE GETTING BUSIER AND BUSIER.

We're all headed in different directions at fast speeds trying to get somewhere. The latest technology allows us to be "plugged in" during most of our waking (and too many of our sleeping) hours, and we are multitasking at every turn. Of course life would be better if we did less, but I don't believe that's going to happen anytime soon. Our hectic lifestyles are negatively impacting our health. Climbing rates of obesity, type 2 diabetes, heart and stroke disease and various cancers are affecting the young and old—our bodies are sending us messages and we need to pay attention. We have to take better care of ourselves if we want to reap the benefits of this incredible world we live in.

Our children's lives are also busy, and when they move away from home they soon find that living a healthy lifestyle is not quite as easy as it used to be. They are suddenly responsible for their own shopping, food preparation, cooking and nutrition. It can be easy for them to make poor choices. As a parent, leading by example when our children are young and helping them to develop healthy habits that they can sustain later on is key to their future success. When you think about it, the eating habits and skills that our children are learning now are laying the groundwork for *their* children's future health. It matters.

The impetus for this book was quite personal. I have two beautiful new grandchildren and I want them to grow healthy and strong. I was struck by the incredible challenges my daughter and son-in-law face as they run their household with two demanding babies. Getting good food on the table is sometimes difficult. While eating well and exercising remain a priority, the temptation for fast and prepared food looms large. As I watch my daughter return to work full time I worry that she will not find quick and healthy meals for her family of four. This book is intended to remedy that concern for her and other families in the same position.

With the recipes in this book and a little bit of planning, you can get delicious, nutritious meals on the table in 30 minutes or less any day of the week (and perhaps even have leftovers for the lunch bag the next day). And because no one wants to be a short-order cook, making separate meals for everyone, I've included tips on how to easily tailor each recipe to the likes and dislikes of even the fussiest eaters: children. Not to forget mom and dad, I've also included useful nutrition tips so you can better understand your diet and lead by example, and the recipes also include at-a-glance labels to help you quickly identify dairy-free 🌀, gluten-free 🌀 and vegetarian 🌱 options.

Living a healthy life, eating well, exercising regularly and spending time with family and friends are what keeps me happy. Helping to inform fellow Canadians on how to improve their health is my passion. Poor diets and lifestyles undercut the quality of life and result in prolonged disease. Doctors' offices and hospitals are filled with chronically sick adults and children who suffer from illnesses that could have been prevented by a healthy lifestyle. The connection between diet and disease has never been more clear, and the argument for improving our diet never more compelling. Improving our diet should be as urgent a matter as treating an epidemic. After all, what we are seeing now *is* an epidemic—an epidemic of poor health related to diet and lifestyle. Eating well starts with educating ourselves first; only then can we teach our family.

Eating fresh fruits and vegetables, lean proteins and complex carbohydrates on a regular basis can keep our bodies fuelled and healthier for years, as well as reduce the risk of—and in some cases even prevent—chronic disease. Making just one healthy change in lifestyle at a time will slowly but surely make a big difference. Addictions—to high-fat, high-sugar and high-sodium processed food—can be broken. Predispositions to chronic diseases can be enormously reduced. Energy levels can be increased. One change at a time, you'll be well on your way to making a healthy diet a habit. This book is brimming with delicious recipes that make putting healthy foods on your plate easy. I'm delighted to present it to you as a useful step in the right direction to a healthy diet.

When you browse through these pages, you'll find recipes for the classics and all the foods you love, with the healthy and tasty twists you've come to expect from me, and all can be made with little fuss. My favourites include Thai Quinoa Salad (page 43); Fresh Tomato Soup with Grilled Cheese Croutons (page 54); Salmon with Pea Pesto (page 118); Prosciutto-Wrapped Chicken Burgers with Sun-dried Tomatoes (page 126); and Gnocchi with Squash, Kale and Parmesan (page 92), just to name a few. I invite you to experiment, make these recipes your own and discover your new favourites.

As always, enjoy!
Rose

APPETIZERS

WHEN MOST PEOPLE think of appetizers, they visualize hors d'oeuvres or fancy finger foods served on platters at parties. But in terms of family meals, many of my appetizers, such as Buffalo Chicken Sliders (page 21) or the Mini Meatball and Cheese Pizzas (page 25), can be served as a first course or the main meal itself. There's no question that many of these appetizers will be a complete meal for kids. If you're serving "appies" before the main meal, just be sure your children don't snack excessively and ruin their appetite for dinner. Appetizer meals can be prepped the day before and then cooked or reheated once you walk in the door.

Instead of potato chips, whip up a batch of Parmesan Kale Chips (page 13) for a crunchy savoury pre-dinner snack. Follow up with my unique but healthier spin on a classic, Mac and Cheese Wonton Cups (page 18). If your kids love poutine, try my nutritious version: Baked Potato Wedges with Chicken Chili (page 23). For burger lovers make the slightly spicy Buffalo Chicken Sliders (page 21) with a side of veggies and dip for a quick and fun meal. Layered dips—Eight-Layer Hummus Dip (page 12) or Seven-Layer Southwest Dip (page 14)—served with either homemade tortilla crisps (page 14) or raw vegetable sticks are fun for the whole family to dig into.

EIGHT-LAYER HUMMUS DIP

Whenever I serve this to my family they devour it—the flavour and texture of this beautiful layered dip is a crowd-pleaser. You can use store-bought hummus or make your own. (Go to my website for the recipe: www.rosereisman.com.) Serve with warmed pita bread cut into wedges or crackers.

PREP TIME:
15
MINUTES

MAKES 4 SERVINGS  **VEGETARIAN**

NUTRITION TIP

Both homemade and store-bought hummus are quite low in calories and fat: 1 Tbsp (15 mL) contains only 20 calories and 1 gram of fat.

FOR KIDS

Most kids love hummus with pita bread. You can customize this dip by omitting any ingredients they may not like, such as the sun-dried tomatoes, red onion and feta. You can also substitute a milder cheese such as cheddar for the feta.

NUTRITIONAL INFORMATION PER SERVING

Calories	184
Carbohydrates	17.1 g
Fibre	2.0 g
Protein	7.8 g
Fat	10.6 g
Saturated Fat	1.9 g
Cholesterol	3 mg
Sodium	343 mg

10 oz (300 g) hummus (store-bought or homemade)
½ cup (125 mL) lightly packed chopped baby spinach leaves
½ cup (125 mL) diced cucumber (unpeeled)
½ cup (125 mL) diced seedless tomatoes
⅓ cup (80 mL) rehydrated sun-dried tomatoes, chopped (see Tip, page 35)
3 Tbsp (45 mL) chopped red onion
3 oz (90 g) crumbled light feta cheese
3 Tbsp (45 mL) chopped pitted black olives

1. Spread the hummus evenly over a serving plate. Sprinkle with even layers of spinach, cucumber, diced tomatoes, sun-dried tomatoes, onion, feta and olives.

TIP To rehydrate sun-dried tomatoes, place in a bowl and cover with boiling water. Set aside for 5 minutes, until softened. Drain well.

PARMESAN KALE CHIPS

If raw kale leaves don't appeal to you, try baked kale chips! These crispy, salty green snacks are trendy for a reason: they are easy to make, incredibly healthy and so delicious! Not to mention that baking the kale instead of deep-frying it retains all of its nutritional benefits. To keep these chips crisp, do not cover them after they are baked. (Pictured with the Black Bean Burger on page 83.)

PREP TIME:
5
MINUTES

COOK TIME:
15
MINUTES

MAKES 8 SERVINGS **GLUTEN FREE**  **VEGETARIAN**

NUTRITION TIP

Kale is a superfood, and 1 cup (250 mL) provides more than your daily needs for vitamin A and vitamin C. Vitamin A is important for eye health, and vitamin C strengthens your immune system. Kale chips are a great low-calorie snack: 1 cup (250 mL) contains only 33 calories, 3 grams of protein and 2.5 grams of fibre.

FOR KIDS

Even kids enjoy this crunchy leafy green snack. Ask them to join you in the kitchen to help you prepare it. It's a great way to educate children about this healthy alternative to the standard potato chip.

1 large bunch green kale, trimmed and thick centre rib removed
2 Tbsp (30 mL) olive oil
2 Tbsp (30 mL) freshly grated Parmesan cheese
Salt and pepper

1. Preheat the oven to 350°F (175°C). Spray 2 large baking sheets with vegetable oil.

2. Tear the kale leaves into bite-size pieces and place in a large bowl. Add the oil, Parmesan, and salt and pepper. Using your hands, massage the leaves for about 2 minutes to soften them. Arrange the leaves in a single layer on the prepared baking sheets.

3. Bake in the preheated oven for 15 minutes or just until crisp. Remove from oven and let cool completely on the baking sheets.

TIP To store chips so they stay crisp, place dry (uncooked) rice in the bottom of an airtight container and then place the cooled kale chips loosely on top. Cover and set aside at room temperature. The rice will absorb any excess moisture. Will keep for up to 1 week.

NUTRITIONAL INFORMATION PER SERVING (1 CUP)

Calories	43
Carbohydrates	0.1 g
Fibre	0.3 g
Protein	0.8 g
Fat	3.9 g
Saturated Fat	0.7 g
Cholesterol	1.1 mg
Sodium	26.3 mg

SEVEN-LAYER SOUTHWEST DIP

Everyone loves the flavours of the Southwest. Make this healthy and filling appetizer for your next party. You can customize it by adding your favourite ingredients, such as diced pitted olives, tomato salsa and even sautéed ground beef or shredded chicken. Serve with baked tortilla chips or sliced fresh vegetables.

PREP TIME:
15
MINUTES

MAKES 8 SERVINGS  GLUTEN FREE   VEGETARIAN

NUTRITION TIP

Rather than serving this dip with pre-packaged deep-fried chips, make your own baked tortilla crisps: Cut a tortilla into 8 triangles. Lightly brush or spray with oil and sprinkle with a little garlic powder, salt, pepper and a hint of cayenne. Bake in a preheated 400°F (200°C) oven just until crisp, 5 to 8 minutes.

FOR KIDS

Kids love dipping into the surprise layers in this fun dish.

NUTRITIONAL INFORMATION PER SERVING

Calories	200
Carbohydrates	21 g
Fibre	7.1 g
Protein	10.5 g
Fat	10 g
Saturated Fat	4 g
Cholesterol	23 mg
Sodium	336 mg

1 can (13 ½ oz/400 mL) refried beans
1 cup (250 mL) reduced-fat sour cream
1 small avocado, halved, pitted, peeled, and diced
1 cup (250 mL) shredded light cheddar cheese, divided
1 cup (250 mL) diced seedless tomato
1 cup (250 mL) canned black beans, rinsed and drained
2 green onions, chopped

1. In a small saucepan over medium heat, heat the refried beans just until warmed through and spreadable, 1 to 2 minutes. (Alternatively, place in a microwave-safe bowl and heat on high for about 45 seconds.) Using a spatula, spread the beans evenly over the bottom of a shallow clear glass bowl.

2. In the following order, spread the remaining fillings over top of the beans in even layers: sour cream, avocado, ¾ cup (185 mL) cheddar cheese, tomato, black beans, remaining ¼ cup (60 mL) cheddar cheese and green onions.

3. If desired, chill dip before serving.

LOADED NACHOS WITH GROUND TURKEY

Loaded nachos—with fried tortilla chips and mounds of cheese sauce, sour cream and ground beef—are an all-time favourite. They may be delicious, but a platter can contain over 2000 calories and 100 grams of fat! Try my tasty and healthier version that uses lean ground turkey and a variety of fresh toppings.

PREP TIME:
15
MINUTES

COOK TIME:
27
MINUTES

MAKES 6 SERVINGS

NUTRITION TIP

Compared with regular ground beef, which contains 300 calories and 20 grams of fat per ½ cup (125 mL), the same amount of ground turkey contains only 125 calories and 7 grams of fat.

FOR KIDS

Kids will love this dish not only for its great taste and texture, but also because they can serve themselves. Omit the jalapeños and cilantro to make it more child-friendly.

NUTRITIONAL INFORMATION PER SERVING

Calories	270
Carbohydrates	21.3 g
Fibre	3.4 g
Protein	16 g
Fat	13 g
Saturated Fat	4.7 g
Cholesterol	47 mg
Sodium	636 mg

2 tsp (10 mL) vegetable oil
1 cup (250 mL) diced onions
1 tsp (5 mL) minced garlic
12 oz (340 g) ground turkey
¾ cup (185 mL) diced red bell pepper
1 tsp (5 mL) chili powder
1 cup (250 mL) canned black beans, rinsed and drained
2 cups (500 mL) tomato sauce (store-bought or homemade)
Salt and pepper
6 to 8 cups (1.5 to 2 L) baked tortilla chips

½ cup (125 mL) shredded light cheddar cheese
½ cup (125 mL) shredded light mozzarella cheese

GARNISHES (OPTIONAL)

2 Tbsp (30 mL) chopped fresh cilantro leaves
2 Tbsp (30 mL) chopped green onions
Reduced-fat sour cream
Thinly sliced jalapeños

1. Preheat the oven to 450°F (230°C). Spray a 10- or 12-inch (25 or 30 cm) pizza pan or large oven-proof platter with vegetable oil.

2. Lightly spray a large skillet with vegetable oil. Set skillet over medium heat and add oil. Add onions and garlic and sauté for about 5 minutes, until softened. Add ground turkey and sauté until no longer pink, about 5 minutes. Add red pepper and sauté for 2 minutes, until softened. Stir in chili powder, black beans, tomato sauce, and salt and pepper. Simmer, uncovered, for 10 minutes, stirring occasionally, until mixture has thickened.

3. Spread half of the tortilla chips evenly over the prepared pan. Pour half of the turkey mixture evenly over top and sprinkle with half of the cheese. Repeat with the remaining chips, turkey mixture and cheese. Bake in the preheated oven for 5 minutes or until the cheese melts and tortillas crisp. Garnish with your choice of toppings (if using) and serve immediately.

MAC AND CHEESE WONTON CUPS

Here's a great way to add some pizzazz to your mac and cheese: Serve individual portions in a crispy cup! Mini meals are trendy, so I decided to pack this classic dish into wonton cups and serve it as a savoury appetizer (it will also work as an entrée served with a diced cooked protein such as chicken or shrimp). Traditionally, this dish contains excessive amounts of calories and fat due to all the butter, cream and excess cheese. In my version, I lighten things up by using a combination of 2% evaporated milk and stock.

PREP TIME:
15
MINUTES

COOK TIME:
18
MINUTES

MAKES 6 SERVINGS  VEGETARIAN

NUTRITION TIPS

Whole-wheat macaroni delivers double the fibre of white pasta. Wonton wrappers contain only 20 calories each, and virtually no fat.

FOR KIDS

These wonton cups are perfect for eating with your hands, and are a definite winner with kids. They will love the mini size, as well as the taste and texture. If desired, omit the sun-dried tomatoes and add green peas or even diced leftover chicken.

12 small (3 ½ inches/9 cm) wonton wrappers
2 Tbsp (30 mL) all-purpose flour
⅓ cup (80 mL) reduced-sodium vegetable or chicken stock
⅓ cup (80 mL) canned 2% evaporated milk
¾ cup (185 mL) shredded light sharp (old) cheddar cheese, divided
8 tsp (40 mL) freshly grated Parmesan cheese, divided
½ tsp (2 mL) Dijon mustard
¾ cup (185 mL) whole-wheat dried macaroni pasta
¼ cup (60 mL) rehydrated sun-dried tomatoes, chopped (see Tip)
2 Tbsp (30 mL) seasoned dry breadcrumbs
1 tsp (5 mL) olive oil
3 Tbsp (45 mL) chopped fresh flat-leaf parsley leaves

1. Preheat the oven to 375°F (190°C). Lightly coat a 12-cup muffin pan with cooking spray.

2. Press 1 wonton wrapper into each cup and lightly spray with vegetable oil. Bake in the preheated oven for 10 minutes or just until lightly browned and crisp. Remove from the oven and set aside. Increase the oven temperature to 425°F (220°C).

3. Meanwhile, in a saucepan, whisk together the flour, stock and milk until smooth. Set the pan over medium heat and cook, whisking constantly, for about 3 minutes or until the mixture has thickened. Stir in ½ cup (125 mL) cheddar, 2 Tbsp (30 mL) Parmesan and the mustard. Cook, stirring constantly, until the cheeses melt, about 1 minute. Remove from the heat and set aside.

4. Meanwhile, bring a large pot of water to a boil. Add the macaroni and cook for 8 to 10 minutes, until tender but still slightly firm (al dente). Drain well and transfer to a large bowl. Add the prepared cheese sauce and the sun-dried tomatoes and toss to combine.

5. Fill each prepared wonton cup with about 3 Tbsp (45 mL) macaroni mixture. Set aside.

6. In a small bowl, combine the breadcrumbs, remaining 2 tsp (10 mL) Parmesan and oil. Sprinkle evenly over the filled wonton cups. Top each with the remaining ¼ cup (60 mL) cheddar cheese.

7. Bake in the center of the preheated oven for 5 minutes or just until the cheese melts. Remove from oven. Garnish with the parsley and serve immediately.

TIP To rehydrate sun-dried tomatoes, place in a bowl and cover with boiling water. Set aside for 5 minutes, until softened. Drain well.

AVOCADO AND CHICKEN WONTON CUPS

The combination of mashed avocado, tender chicken morsels and a crunchy wonton wrapper makes the perfect pop-in-your-mouth appie! Wonton wrappers are available in the produce section of your supermarket. Don't confuse them with egg roll wrappers—wonton wrappers are thinner.

MAKES 12 SERVINGS

PREP TIME:
10
MINUTES

COOK TIME:
20
MINUTES

NUTRITION TIP

Baking wonton wrappers instead of deep-frying them saves calories and fat. One wonton wrapper contains only 23 calories and virtually no fat. Fried wontons contain double the calories and about 4 grams of fat each.

FOR KIDS

Omit the cilantro, and use a milder cheese, such as mozzarella or mild cheddar.

NUTRITIONAL INFORMATION PER SERVING (1 WONTON CUP)

Calories	81
Carbohydrates	7.0 g
Fibre	1.4 g
Protein	5.8 g
Fat	3.6 g
Saturated Fat	0.8 g
Cholesterol	12 mg
Sodium	84 mg

12 small (3 ½ inches/9 cm) wonton wrappers
1 avocado, halved, pitted and peeled
3 Tbsp (45 mL) fresh lemon or lime juice
2 Tbsp (30 mL) chopped fresh cilantro leaves
1 Tbsp (15 mL) reduced-fat mayonnaise
1 clove garlic
¼ tsp (1 mL) ground cumin

3 Tbsp (45 mL) finely diced red onion
1 cup (250 mL) finely diced cooked boneless skinless chicken breast
¼ cup (60 mL) diced seedless tomato
⅓ cup (80 mL) shredded white cheddar or Monterey Jack cheese

1. Preheat the oven to 375°F (190°C). Lightly spray a 12-cup mini muffin pan with vegetable oil.

2. Press 1 wonton wrapper into each cup. Lightly spray with vegetable oil and bake in the preheated oven for 10 minutes or just until lightly browned and crisp. Remove from oven and set aside.

3. In bowl, using a fork, mash together the avocado, lemon juice, cilantro, mayonnaise, garlic and cumin until smooth. (Alternatively, use a mini food processor.) Stir in the onion, chicken and tomato.

4. Divide mixture evenly among wonton cups and sprinkle with cheese. Serve immediately.

BUFFALO CHICKEN SLIDERS

These mini chicken burgers make a great appetizer for a gathering or a complete meal when served with a side of veggies or a salad. If you want to reduce the calories and carbs, just serve on half a bun or on its own. You can also substitute lean ground beef or pork. Sriracha is a hot sauce made from chili peppers, distilled vinegar, garlic, sugar and salt. You can substitute any hot sauce you like.

MAKES 12 SERVINGS

PREP TIME:
10
MINUTES

COOK TIME:
12
MINUTES

NUTRITION TIP

The red chili peppers in Sriracha contain capsaicin, which is known to help boost metabolism and aid in weight loss.

FOR KIDS

My advice is to leave out the hot sauce! You can also swap ketchup for the ranch dressing, if your children prefer it.

NUTRITIONAL INFORMATION PER SERVING (1 SLIDER)

Calories	211
Carbohydrates	20 g
Fibre	0.3 g
Protein	10.9 g
Fat	10.1 g
Saturated Fat	1.0 g
Cholesterol	48 mg
Sodium	277 mg

1 lb (500 g) ground chicken or turkey
⅓ cup (80 mL) unseasoned dry breadcrumbs
3 Tbsp (45 mL) finely chopped green onions
3 Tbsp (45 mL) finely chopped fresh cilantro or basil leaves
1 egg
¼ cup (60 mL) Sriracha or your favourite hot sauce

1 Tbsp (15 mL) olive oil
1½ tsp (7 mL) minced garlic
Salt and pepper
½ cup (125 mL) shredded light sharp (old) cheddar cheese
12 mini hamburger buns
¼ cup (60 mL) light ranch dressing or reduced-fat mayonnaise
12 thin slices plum tomato

1. In a large bowl, combine chicken, breadcrumbs, onions, cilantro, egg, Sriracha, oil, garlic, and salt and pepper, stirring well. Using your hands, form 12 mini burger patties (about 2 oz/60 g each).

2. Preheat a grill pan or skillet over medium heat. Lightly spray with vegetable oil. Cook burgers for about 10 minutes, turning halfway, until cooked through (internal temperature should reach 165°F/74°C when tested with a cooking thermometer).

3. Sprinkle cooked patties with cheese, cover and heat just until cheese has melted, about 2 minutes.

4. Split open buns. On bottom half, spread some ranch dressing. Top with cheese burger and tomato slice. Cover with other half of bun. Serve immediately.

BAKED POTATO WEDGES WITH CHICKEN CHILI

For this dish, I serve my chicken chili over potato wedges, then sprinkle it with shredded cheese. It's a healthy, complete and hearty one-dish meal.

PREP TIME:
10
MINUTES

COOK TIME:
20
MINUTES

MAKES 6 SERVINGS

NUTRITION TIP

Compared with 8 ounces (230 g) of deep-fried French fries, which contain approximately 700 calories and 35 grams of fat, an equal amount of baked potato wedges contain only 270 calories and 8 grams of fat.

FOR KIDS

Before baking, cut potatoes into thinner wedges for smaller children. Omit the jalapeño pepper.

NUTRITIONAL INFORMATION PER SERVING
(4 WEDGES + ½ CUP CHILI)

Calories	323
Carbohydrates	41 g
Fibre	5 g
Protein	17 g
Fat	8 g
Saturated Fat	9 g
Cholesterol	37 mg
Sodium	322 mg

POTATO WEDGES

3 large baking potatoes (about 2 lb/1 kg)

2 Tbsp (30 mL) olive oil

½ tsp (2 mL) garlic powder

2 Tbsp (30 mL) freshly grated Parmesan cheese

¼ tsp (1 mL) chili powder

CHICKEN CHILI

6 oz (175 g) boneless skinless chicken breast, diced (about 1½ single breast pieces)

2 Tbsp (30 mL) all-purpose flour

2 tsp (10 mL) vegetable oil, divided

¾ cup (185 mL) chopped onion

½ cup (125 mL) canned corn kernels, rinsed and drained

1 tsp (5 mL) minced garlic

¾ cup (185 mL) canned black beans, rinsed and drained

1¼ cups (310 mL) tomato sauce (store-bought or homemade)

½ cup (125 mL) reduced-sodium chicken stock

1½ tsp (7 mL) chili powder

1 tsp (5 mL) seeded and finely chopped jalapeño pepper

Salt and pepper

TOPPING

½ cup (125 mL) shredded light mozzarella cheese

1. **Prepare potato wedges:** Preheat the oven to 425°F (220°C). Lightly coat a rimmed baking sheet with cooking spray.

2. Cut each potato lengthwise into 8 wedges. Place on the prepared baking sheet. Brush the oil over both sides of the wedges.

3. In a small bowl, combine the garlic powder, Parmesan and chili powder. Sprinkle over both sides of the potato wedges.

RECIPE CONTINUED ON NEXT PAGE

BAKED POTATO WEDGES WITH CHICKEN CHILI CONTINUED

4. Bake in the middle of the preheated oven for 20 to 25 minutes, until tender and browned, turning over after 15 minutes.

5. **Prepare chicken chili:** Meanwhile, in a bowl, combine the chicken and flour and toss to coat well. Lightly coat a non-stick saucepan with cooking spray, add 1 tsp (5 mL) of the vegetable oil and set over medium heat. Sauté the chicken until lightly browned and cooked through, about 5 minutes. Using a slotted spoon, transfer the cooked chicken to a plate.

6. Lightly coat the same saucepan with cooking spray. Add the remaining vegetable oil and set over medium heat. Add the onion, corn and garlic and cook, stirring occasionally, until the corn is lightly browned, about 5 minutes.

7. Stir in the beans, tomato sauce, stock, chili powder, jalapeño, and salt and pepper. Bring to a boil, reduce the heat and simmer, covered, for 10 minutes. Return the diced chicken to the pan and cook until heated through, 1 to 2 minutes.

8. Divide cooked potato wedges among serving plates. Top with the chicken chili and sprinkle with cheese. Serve immediately.

MINI MEATBALL AND CHEESE PIZZAS

This pizza is inspired by a classic—spaghetti and meatballs—and is given a delicious twist by substituting naan bread for the pizza crust. Naan bread has a soft texture and is tastier than regular pizza dough. If you prefer, you can use a fresh or frozen pizza crust. Mini pizza makes a great party appetizer, but can also be served with a side salad for an easy weeknight dinner.

PREP TIME:
15
MINUTES

COOK TIME:
20
MINUTES

MAKES 8 SERVINGS

NUTRITION TIP

There is a big difference between extra lean, lean, medium and regular ground beef in terms of calories and fat. Regular ground beef has a maximum fat content of 30%; medium 23%; lean 17%; and extra lean 10%. For the best flavour, I always use lean ground beef. If using extra lean ground beef, add 1 Tbsp (15 mL) of olive oil to the mixture to aid browning.

FOR KIDS

Let children assist you in the kitchen when making these pizzas—rolling the mini meatballs is always fun!

NUTRITIONAL INFORMATION PER SERVING (¼ PIZZA)

Calories	178
Carbohydrates	20 g
Fibre	0.8 g
Protein	9.2 g
Fat	6.5 g
Saturated Fat	2.2 g
Cholesterol	33 mg
Sodium	413 mg

MEATBALLS
¼ lb (120 g) lean ground beef
2 Tbsp (30 mL) unseasoned dry breadcrumbs
1 Tbsp (15 mL) finely chopped green onions
1 Tbsp (15 mL) barbeque sauce
1 small egg
½ tsp (2 mL) minced garlic
½ cup (125 mL) tomato sauce (store-bought or homemade)
2 round naan breads
3 oz (90 g) shredded light mozzarella cheese
2 Tbsp (30 mL) chopped fresh basil leaves

1. Preheat the oven to 425°F (220°C). Lightly spray a baking sheet or pizza pan with vegetable oil.

2. In a large bowl, combine ground beef, breadcrumbs, onions, barbeque sauce, egg and garlic. Using your hands, form about 20 mini meatballs (about 1 Tbsp/15 mL each).

3. Using the back of a spoon or a brush, spread tomato sauce over naan. Scatter meatballs over top and sprinkle with cheese. Bake in the preheated oven for 15 to 20 minutes or until the naan is browned around the edges and crisp and the cheese is melted and the meatballs are cooked through. Remove from the oven and garnish with the basil. Serve.

MEATBALL AND RICE NOODLE LETTUCE WRAPS

In Asian cuisine we often see soft lettuce leaves being used as wraps for food, such as in moo shu pork. Here, I build on this idea by combining Asian-spiced mini meatballs with a delicious light coconut sauce and serving it over a bed of rice noodles plated atop a Boston lettuce leaf. You can wrap and eat it taco-style or use a fork and knife. It's a fun meal to enjoy any night of the week and a tasty alternative to serve guests when entertaining.

PREP TIME:
20 MINUTES

COOK TIME:
15 MINUTES

MAKES 10 SERVINGS **DAIRY FREE**

NUTRITION TIP

The red chili peppers in Sriracha contain capsaicin, which is known to boost metabolism and aid in weight loss.

FOR KIDS

Some children can tolerate Sriracha, since once the red peppers are processed they lose much of their heat, but if they aren't yet familiar with the flavour, it's a good idea to use half the amount to start.

NUTRITIONAL INFORMATION PER SERVING (1 WRAP)

Calories	131
Carbohydrates	11 g
Fibre	0.5 g
Protein	10 g
Fat	4 g
Saturated Fat	2 g
Cholesterol	42 mg
Sodium	225 mg

SAUCE
¾ cup (185 mL) canned light coconut milk
⅓ cup (80 mL) reduced-sodium beef or chicken stock
2 tsp (10 mL) fresh lemon juice
2 Tbsp (30 mL) hoisin sauce
2 tsp (10 mL) packed brown sugar
1 tsp (5 mL) cornstarch
1 tsp (5 mL) minced peeled fresh ginger
1 tsp (5 mL) minced garlic
1 tsp (5 mL) Sriracha or your favourite hot sauce

MEATBALLS
1 lb (500 g) extra lean ground beef
1 egg
¼ cup (60 mL) hoisin sauce
¼ cup (60 mL) finely diced green onions
¼ cup (60 mL) unseasoned dry breadcrumbs
2 Tbsp (30 mL) finely chopped fresh cilantro leaves
2 tsp (10 mL) minced garlic
1½ tsp (7 mL) minced peeled fresh ginger
Salt and pepper
2 oz (60 g) dried thin rice noodles
10 Boston lettuce leaves

GARNISH (OPTIONAL)
¼ cup (60 mL) diced red bell pepper
2 tsp (10 mL) toasted sesame seeds (see Tip, page 35)

1. Preheat the oven to 425°F (220°C). Line a baking sheet with foil and lightly spray with vegetable oil.

2. **Make the sauce:** In a bowl, combine the coconut milk, stock, lemon juice, hoisin, sugar, cornstarch, ginger, garlic and Sriracha and stir until the cornstarch is dissolved. Set aside.

RECIPE CONTINUED ON NEXT PAGE

MEATBALL AND RICE NOODLE LETTUCE WRAPS CONTINUED

3. **Make the meatballs:** In a bowl, combine the beef, egg, hoisin, onions, breadcrumbs, cilantro, garlic, ginger, and salt and pepper. Using your hands, form about thirty 1-inch (2.5 cm) meatballs. Place on the prepared baking sheet and bake in the preheated oven for 10 minutes or until internal temperature reaches 165°F (74°C) when tested with a cooking thermometer.

4. In a small skillet over medium heat, cook the prepared sauce until slightly thickened, about 2 minutes.

5. Meanwhile, in a saucepan of boiling water, cook the noodles according to the package instructions. Drain well.

6. Top each lettuce leaf with an equal amount of the cooked noodles. Top noodles with 3 meatballs and drizzle with the sauce. Garnish with the red pepper and a sprinkling of sesame seeds.

TIP You can buy toasted sesame seeds at most supermarkets or toast them yourself: Place them in a dry skillet over medium heat, stirring constantly, until lightly browned, about 3 minutes.

SALADS

SALADS USED TO be the part of a meal we felt compelled to eat in order to meet our daily quota of vegetables, but no more. With some attention to the right mix of ingredients, a salad can be a complete and satisfying meal in its own right. To make the perfect main-course salad, include a balance of vegetables, fruit, lean protein, whole grains, small amounts of cheese, and beans or legumes, and dress with a light and tasty dressing.

Dressings too have evolved. I use a variety of oils, vinegars, citrus fruit and other juices, mustards and spices to add more flavour with fewer calories and less fat. When I want a sweeter dressing I often add maple syrup or cider vinegar, such as in Sweet Potato, Cranberry and Quinoa Salad with Maple Dressing (page 42). I also love using ginger in my dressings, as in Bok Choy and Mandarin Orange Salad with Ginger Dressing (page 34). The honey dressing in Thai Quinoa Salad (page 43) is perfect.

When choosing leafy greens, keep in mind that darker greens (such as kale, spinach, arugula and bok choy) are more nutritious than lighter greens (such as iceberg and Boston bibb). I like to use lighter greens as a garnish.

What's wonderful about the salads in this chapter is that you can use them as a starting point, substitute your favourite ingredients and create an entirely new recipe. While I can't play favourites—each of the salads included in this chapter is so tasty—be sure to try Baby Kale, Butternut Squash and Pomegranate Salad (page 31) and Barley Lentil Salad (page 40). Both are delicious, nutritious full-course meals.

BABY KALE, BUTTERNUT SQUASH AND POMEGRANATE SALAD

The combination of the baby kale, sweet squash, berries and pomegranate seeds makes this an exceptional salad—not only in taste and appearance, but in health benefits. I love to top it with some cooked chicken, fish or beef and serve it as a main course. Pomegranate juice can be refrigerated for up to 10 days and frozen for up to 1 year.

PREP TIME:
5
MINUTES

COOK TIME:
5
MINUTES

MAKES 6 SERVINGS    DAIRY FREE    GLUTEN FREE   🌿 VEGETARIAN

NUTRITION TIP

This salad explodes with nutrients. The baby kale contains protein and fibre, and 1 cup (250 mL) of cooked squash delivers over 450% of your total daily needs for vitamin A, which helps to build a stronger immune system.

FOR KIDS

This salad is so versatile. You can substitute any of the fruits and vegetables for your children's favourites. Try cooked sweet potatoes instead of the butternut squash, and be sure to cut it into very small cubes, which is more appealing to kids.

1 cup (250 mL) diced butternut squash (see Tip)
8 cups (2 L) lightly packed baby kale or spinach leaves
⅓ cup (80 mL) diced unsulphured dried apricots
⅓ cup (80 mL) pomegranate seeds
½ cup (125 mL) fresh blueberries or raspberries

DRESSING
¼ cup (60 mL) pomegranate juice
2 ½ Tbsp (37 mL) extra virgin olive oil
1 Tbsp (15 mL) balsamic vinegar
2 tsp (10 mL) liquid honey

1. In a small saucepan, boil the squash for 5 minutes or just until tender. Drain well and set aside for about 10 minutes, until cool.

2. **Make the dressing:** In a small bowl, whisk together the pomegranate juice, oil, vinegar and honey. Set aside.

3. Arrange the kale on a serving plate. Sprinkle with the apricots, pomegranate seeds, berries and cooled cooked squash. Pour prepared dressing over top and toss until well coated. Serve.

TIP For speed, purchase pre-peeled and seeded packaged squash.

NUTRITIONAL INFORMATION PER SERVING

Calories	151
Carbohydrates	23.3 g
Fibre	4.0 g
Protein	3.6 g
Fat	6.4 g
Saturated Fat	0.9 g
Cholesterol	0 mg
Sodium	46.7 mg

TOMATO, PESTO AND BUFFALO MOZZARELLA SALAD

Ripe tomatoes, garlicky pesto and creamy Buffalo mozzarella cheese combine to make a delicious appetizer, salad or side dish to accompany any Italian entrée. The key to best flavour is to use ripe field tomatoes, as their size works perfectly with the sliced mozzarella, but you can also use ripe plum or vine tomatoes. Buffalo mozzarella is made from the milk of the water buffalo and comes packed in water. It's high in protein and calcium. If you're not using the whole piece, the rest can be stored in the liquid it came with. If you can't find Buffalo mozzarella, you can substitute bocconcini or mozzarella cheese with good results.

PREP TIME:
15
MINUTES

MAKES 4 SERVINGS  GLUTEN FREE VEGETARIAN

NUTRITION TIP
Tomatoes contain three high-powered antioxidants: beta-carotene, which delivers vitamin A to the body, and vitamin E and vitamin C. These antioxidants may reduce the risk of pancreatic cancer.

FOR KIDS
To make this dish friendly to little fingers, substitute whole sweet cherry or grape tomatoes for the field tomatoes. In place of the Buffalo mozzarella, shred some mozzarella cheese over top or use baby bocconcini.

1 large ripe field tomato, sliced into six to eight ¼-inch (6 mm) slices
2 Tbsp (30 mL) basil pesto (store-bought or homemade; recipe follows)
2 oz (60 g) Buffalo mozzarella or bocconcini cheese, sliced into 8 small rounds
6 fresh basil leaves, for garnish

1. Place 1 slice of the tomato on the outer edge of a serving plate. Spread about 1 tsp (5 mL) of pesto on top of the tomato. About halfway down the tomato slice, lay a slice of cheese. Repeat with the remaining tomato, pesto and cheese, alternating the layers across the plate. Refrigerate remaining pesto. Garnish with the basil leaves. Serve.

BASIL PESTO

This is my go-to pesto recipe, which is lower in calories, fat and sodium than commercial brands. It's extremely versatile: Substitute any of your favourite herbs or leafy greens for the basil (cilantro, parsley, spinach, kale or arugula all work well). Stir it into cooked grains or vegetables, or spoon it over your favourite protein.

MAKES ¾ CUP (185 ML)

1 cup (250 mL) packed fresh basil leaves
2 Tbsp (30 mL) freshly grated Parmesan cheese
2 Tbsp (30 mL) light cream cheese
2 Tbsp (30 mL) extra virgin olive oil
3 Tbsp (45 mL) water or reduced-sodium stock
1 Tbsp (15 mL) toasted pine nuts (see Tip, page 35)

1. In a small food processor, combine all of the ingredients. Purée until smooth. If the mixture is too thick, add water, a tablespoon at a time, until the desired consistency is reached. Pesto will keep in an airtight container in the refrigerator for up to 7 days and in the freezer for up to 4 months.

TIP To toast pine nuts, place in a dry skillet over medium-high heat and cook, stirring continuously, just until lightly browned. Remove from pan immediately and set aside to cool slightly before using.

BOK CHOY AND MANDARIN ORANGE SALAD WITH GINGER DRESSING

Bok choy is usually eaten cooked in stir-fries, but it's absolutely delicious served raw in this salad, paired with sweet dried cranberries and mandarin segments and a true Asian dressing.

PREP TIME:
15
MINUTES

MAKES 6 SERVINGS   **DAIRY FREE**   **VEGETARIAN**

NUTRITION TIP

Bok choy is one of the lowest-calorie and lowest-carb vegetables there is: It contains only 20 calories and 11 grams of carbohydrates per 1 cup (250 mL). One cup also gives you 75% of your recommended daily intake of vitamin C, which will help to boost your immune system. The nutrients are best maintained when eaten raw, so put this salad in your regular rotation!

FOR KIDS

Bok choy can seem slightly bitter to children, so slice it very thinly to help them develop a taste for it. You can also reduce the quantity of the ginger by half and increase the amount of sugar slightly to make the dressing more appealing to children's taste buds.

12 oz (340 g) baby bok choy, trimmed and chopped

2 green onions, chopped

⅓ cup (80 mL) dried unsweetened cranberries

½ cup (125 mL) mandarin segments (fresh or canned; drain if canned)

¼ cup (60 mL) toasted sliced blanched almonds (see Tip)

3 Tbsp (45 mL) chopped fresh cilantro or flat-leaf parsley leaves

DRESSING

⅓ cup (80 mL) minced red onion

2 ½ Tbsp (37 mL) vegetable oil

2 ½ Tbsp (37 mL) rice wine vinegar

2 ½ Tbsp (37 mL) water

1 ½ Tbsp (22 mL) ketchup

1 Tbsp (15 mL) minced peeled fresh ginger

1 Tbsp (15 mL) reduced-sodium soy sauce

1 ½ tsp (7 mL) sesame oil

1 ½ tsp (7 mL) granulated sugar

1 ½ tsp (7 mL) fresh lemon juice

1. Combine the bok choy, green onions, cranberries and mandarins on a serving platter. Garnish with the almonds and cilantro. Set aside.

2. In a small bowl, whisk together the onion, vegetable oil, vinegar, water, ketchup, ginger, soy sauce, sesame oil, sugar and lemon juice. (Alternatively, purée in a small food processor until smooth.)

3. Pour over the salad and toss until the bok choy is well coated. Serve immediately.

NUTRITIONAL INFORMATION PER SERVING

Calories	146
Carbohydrates	14.0 g
Fibre	2.2 g
Protein	2.6 g
Fat	9.6 g
Saturated Fat	0.8 g
Cholesterol	0 mg
Sodium	169 mg

TIP To toast nuts or seeds, place in a dry skillet over medium-high heat and cook, stirring continuously, for about 2 minutes, until lightly brown. Remove from pan immediately and set aside to cool slightly before using.

DRESSING YOUR SALAD

To keep your greens crunchy, do not dress a salad until ready to eat. The only exception is large kale leaves, which must be massaged and dressed before eating to make them tender. It's best to seed tomatoes to avoid excess moisture, which will water down your dressing. Don't add cucumbers, tomatoes or any vegetable with a high water content until the salad is ready to serve.

GREEK SALAD WITH ROASTED POTATOES

Traditional potato salads prepared with mayonnaise-based dressings contain loads of calories and fat. In this take on a classic, I combine roasted baby potatoes with tomatoes, cucumber and feta cheese for a Mediterranean flare. Roasting the potatoes gives them a crunchy texture that's more appealing to children (and adults).

PREP TIME:
5
MINUTES

COOK TIME:
20
MINUTES

MAKES 8 SERVINGS    GLUTEN FREE   VEGETARIAN

NUTRITION TIP

French fries and potato chips aside, potatoes are a healthy, low-calorie, high-fibre vegetable that offer protection against heart disease and cancer. They're a very good source of vitamin B_6 and a good source of potassium, vitamin C and dietary fibre.

FOR KIDS

To appeal to a child's tastes, dice all the vegetables, since kids often prefer to eat small pieces of food. You can substitute the feta cheese with diced mozzarella, mild cheddar or Havarti cheese. Omit the red onion or replace it with chopped green onion.

NUTRITIONAL INFORMATION PER SERVING

Calories	153
Carbohydrates	18.8 g
Fibre	2.6 g
Protein	4.6 g
Fat	6.9 g
Saturated Fat	1.7 g
Cholesterol	3.1 mg
Sodium	196 mg

1¼ lb (625 g) baby red potatoes, quartered

¼ tsp (1 mL) chili powder

¼ tsp (1 mL) garlic powder

1½ cups (375 mL) cubed (1 inch/2.5 cm) plum tomatoes, with juice

1½ cups (375 mL) cubed (1 inch/2.5 cm) English cucumber (unpeeled)

1 cup (250 mL) cubed (1 inch/2.5 cm) red bell pepper

⅓ cup (80 mL) diced red onion

¼ cup (60 mL) diced pitted black olives (optional)

3 oz (90 g) crumbled light feta cheese

3 Tbsp (45 mL) extra virgin olive oil

3 Tbsp (45 mL) fresh lemon juice

1 tsp (5 mL) minced garlic

Salt and pepper

¼ cup (60 mL) chopped fresh oregano or basil leaves

1. Preheat the oven to 450°F (230°C). Line a baking sheet with foil and lightly spray with vegetable oil.

2. Arrange the potatoes in a single layer on the prepared baking sheet. Sprinkle with chili and garlic powders. Lightly spray with vegetable oil. Bake in the preheated oven for 15 minutes or just until tender.

3. Meanwhile, in a large bowl, combine the tomatoes, cucumber, red pepper, onion, olives (if using), cheese, oil, lemon juice, garlic, salt and pepper and oregano. Add the baked potatoes and toss to combine. Serve.

MIDDLE EASTERN CHICKPEA SALAD

Chickpeas, also known as garbanzo beans, are a classic ingredient in Middle Eastern cuisine (hummus, tagines, salads and stews). In this dish, I make them the star of the show. Serve this salad with the baked pita wedges, which are great for scooping up the salad or just munching on alongside.

MAKES 6 SERVINGS  **VEGETARIAN**

PREP TIME:
15
MINUTES

COOK TIME:
5
MINUTES

NUTRITION TIP

Chickpeas are high in fibre and protein and have a low glycemic index, which means they raise your blood sugar slowly, which in turn stabilizes blood sugar levels. You can eliminate one-third of the sodium in canned chickpeas simply by rinsing them thoroughly under cold water before using.

FOR KIDS

For a child's taste buds try substituting the tahini for peanut or almond butter. Also, dice the vegetables, since kids prefer small mouthfuls.

NUTRITIONAL INFORMATION PER SERVING

Calories	370
Carbohydrates	59.4 g
Fibre	6.8 g
Protein	12.9 g
Fat	10.9 g
Saturated Fat	1.6 g
Cholesterol	2.6 mg
Sodium	550 mg

PITA WEDGES
1 large (6 ½ inches/17 cm) whole-wheat pita
⅛ tsp (0.5 mL) chili powder
Salt and pepper

SALAD
⅓ cup (80 mL) reduced-fat mayonnaise
3 Tbsp (45 mL) plain 1% yogurt
4 tsp (20 mL) sesame oil
4 tsp (20 mL) reduced-sodium soy sauce
1 Tbsp (15 mL) tahini
1 Tbsp (15 mL) water
1 can (15 oz/444 mL) chickpeas, drained and rinsed
2 cups (500 mL) cubed seeded plum tomatoes
2 cups (500 mL) cubed English cucumber (unpeeled)
2 green onions, chopped
⅓ cup (80 mL) chopped fresh cilantro or mint leaves

1. **Make the pita wedges:** Preheat the oven to 425°F (220°C). Set aside a baking sheet.

2. Cut the pita into 4 even wedges, then slice the wedges horizontally to make 8 wedges total. Lightly spray pita with vegetable oil. Sprinkle with the chili powder and salt and pepper. Spread in a single layer on the baking sheet and bake in the preheated oven for 5 minutes or just until lightly browned and crisp. Remove from oven and let cool on sheet.

3. **Make the salad:** In a small bowl, whisk together the mayonnaise, yogurt, sesame oil, soy sauce, tahini and water until smooth.

4. On a serving platter, combine the chickpeas, tomatoes, cucumber, green onions and cilantro. Toss with the prepared dressing, and season with salt and pepper. Serve with baked pita wedges.

COOKING DRIED CHICKPEAS

To use dried chickpeas instead of canned, bring a pot full of water with ⅔ cup (160 mL) dried chickpeas to a boil for 2 minutes. Remove from the heat and let sit, covered in water, for 1 hour. Drain, cover with fresh water, and simmer for about 30 minutes or just until tender.

DATE AND ORANGE ARUGULA SALAD WITH POMEGRANATE DRESSING

Slightly spicy arugula goes especially well with sweet dates and a pomegranate dressing. The best-tasting dates are fresh Medjool dates. You can find them in well-stocked supermarkets and specialty food stores. (Store them in an airtight container in a cool, dark place for up to 4 weeks.) If you can't find fresh dates, use dried dates, but soak them in a bowl of hot water for 5 minutes to soften them (drain well before using). Look for pure pomegranate juice with no added sugar (it will keep, refrigerated, for up to 1 week).

PREP TIME:
15
MINUTES

MAKES 6 SERVINGS **DAIRY FREE** **GLUTEN FREE** **VEGETARIAN**

NUTRITION TIP

Dates are a source of antioxidants and a low-glycemic food (despite their naturally sweet taste), making them good for balancing blood pressure and blood sugar. They are also a good source of fibre and potassium.

FOR KIDS

If your children don't enjoy dates, try grapes or dried unsweetened cranberries. Omit the onion, if desired. You can always use romaine lettuce instead of the arugula, which some kids find too bitter.

8 cups (2 L) lightly packed arugula or spinach
4 fresh dates, pitted and quartered (see Tip)
⅓ cup (80 mL) thinly sliced red onion
1 orange, peeled and sliced into 6 rounds, then rounds halved
⅓ cup (80 mL) toasted sliced pecan halves (see Tips, page 35)

DRESSING
3 Tbsp (45 mL) pure pomegranate juice
1½ Tbsp (22 mL) extra virgin olive oil
4 tsp (20 mL) balsamic vinegar
1½ tsp (7 mL) liquid honey
Salt and pepper

1. Arrange the arugula on a large serving platter. Top with dates, onions, orange and pecans. Set aside.

2. In a small bowl, whisk together the pomegranate juice, oil, vinegar, honey, and salt and pepper. Drizzle over salad and serve.

TIP If you can't find fresh dates, you can substitute an equal amount of dried figs or raisins.

NUTRITIONAL INFORMATION PER SERVING

Calories	115
Carbohydrates	11.9 g
Fibre	1.8 g
Protein	1.7 g
Fat	7.5 g
Saturated Fat	0.8 g
Cholesterol	0 mg
Sodium	58 mg

BARLEY LENTIL SALAD

If you've ever tried black beluga lentils you may never go back to regular lentils again. They resemble beluga caviar and have a less earthy taste than green lentils. You can find them in well-stocked supermarkets, health-food stores and bulk food stores.

PREP TIME:
5
MINUTES

COOK TIME:
25
MINUTES

MAKES 6 SERVINGS  **VEGETARIAN**

NUTRITION TIP

Black lentils contain antioxidants that stop free radical damage, which may protect against cancer and heart disease.

FOR KIDS

If your kids don't like lentils of any sort, you can substitute an equal amount of canned chickpeas (rinsed and drained), which children often prefer.

NUTRITIONAL INFORMATION PER SERVING

Calories	253
Carbohydrates	28.4 g
Fibre	8.0 g
Protein	10.9 g
Fat	11.8 g
Saturated Fat	2.5 g
Cholesterol	4.2 mg
Sodium	279.5 mg

½ cup (125 mL) black beluga lentils or green lentils, rinsed and drained
½ cup (125 mL) pearl barley
1 tsp (5 mL) minced garlic
2 ½ cups (625 mL) lightly packed finely chopped kale or spinach
3 oz (90 g) crumbled light feta cheese
⅓ cup (80 mL) finely chopped red onion
3 Tbsp (45 mL) extra virgin olive oil
3 Tbsp (45 mL) fresh lemon juice
1 tsp (5 mL) Dijon mustard
⅓ cup (80 mL) toasted sliced blanched almonds (see Tip, page 35)
Salt and pepper

1. Bring 2 small saucepans of water to a boil. In one pan, add the lentils. Add the barley to the other pan. Return each pot to a boil, cover, reduce the heat to medium and simmer for 20 to 25 minutes or until the barley and lentils are tender. Drain and rinse under cold running water until completely cooled. Transfer to one serving bowl.

2. Add garlic, kale, feta, onion, oil, juice, mustard, almonds, and salt and pepper. Toss until well combined. Serve.

SWEET POTATO, CRANBERRY AND QUINOA SALAD WITH MAPLE DRESSING

Quinoa, the most popular ancient grain, is actually a seed. It is a complete protein, which means it contains all of the essential amino acids. It's a great substitute for meat, poultry or fish. This dish works equally well as a main course or a side dish. The sweet potatoes, dried cranberries and maple syrup dressing are a perfect match for the slightly chewy texture of the quinoa.

PREP TIME:
15
MINUTES

COOK TIME:
15
MINUTES

MAKES 6 SERVINGS **DAIRY FREE**  **GLUTEN FREE** **VEGETARIAN**

NUTRITION TIP

Sweet potatoes contain antioxidants that have anti-inflammatory properties. The beta-carotene and vitamin C in this vegetable helps to eliminate cancer-friendly free radicals.

FOR KIDS

If your kids don't like the taste and texture of quinoa, substitute an equal quantity of white rice or brown rice (if using brown rice, increase the amount of stock to 2 cups/500 mL).

NUTRITIONAL INFORMATION PER SERVING

Calories	237
Carbohydrates	35.8 g
Fibre	3.6 g
Protein	7.1 g
Fat	8.1 g
Saturated Fat	1.2 g
Cholesterol	0 mg
Sodium	82.1 mg

QUINOA SALAD

1 medium sweet potato, peeled and cut into 1-inch (2.5 cm) cubes

1 cup (250 mL) quinoa, rinsed and drained

1½ cups (375 mL) reduced-sodium vegetable or chicken stock

½ cup (125 mL) dried unsweetened cranberries

¼ cup (60 mL) finely sliced green onions

¼ cup (60 mL) chopped fresh cilantro or basil leaves

¼ cup (60 mL) unsalted roasted pepitas (pumpkin seeds) (see Tip, page 35)

Salt and pepper

DRESSING

½ tsp (2 mL) minced garlic

¼ tsp (1 mL) Dijon mustard

1½ tsp (7 mL) apple cider vinegar

4 tsp (20 mL) pure maple syrup

1½ Tbsp (22 mL) extra virgin olive oil

2 tsp (10 mL) fresh lemon juice

1. **Make the salad:** Preheat the oven to 425°F (220°C). Lightly spray a baking sheet with vegetable oil.

2. Arrange the sweet potato cubes in a single layer on the prepared baking sheet. Roast in the preheated oven for 15 minutes or just until tender.

3. Meanwhile, in a saucepan, combine the quinoa and stock. Bring to a boil, cover, reduce the heat to low and simmer for 15 minutes, until the quinoa is light and fluffy and the water has been absorbed. Remove from the heat and set aside, covered, to absorb any remaining liquid.

4. Transfer the cooked quinoa to a serving bowl. Add the roasted sweet potatoes, dried cranberries, green onions, cilantro, pepitas, and salt and pepper. Set aside.

5. **Make the dressing:** In a bowl, whisk together the garlic, mustard, vinegar, maple syrup, olive oil and lemon juice. Add to the quinoa salad and toss until well coated. Serve.

THAI QUINOA SALAD

I eat quinoa on a weekly basis and love to experiment with different applications. This light peanut butter and sesame dressing adds an incredible Thai flavour to this salad. Making this a day ahead and refrigerating it before serving actually enhances the flavour. The quinoa delivers a vegetable source of protein, but if desired you can add some leftover diced chicken or meat.

MAKES 6 SERVINGS **DAIRY FREE**

NUTRITION TIP

For those with allergies, you can make the dressing with Wow Butter, which is peanut- and tree nut-free, dairy-free and egg-free. It is actually more nutritious than peanut butter because it is a complete protein. It is also a good source of omega-3 essential fatty acids.

FOR KIDS

This is a great way to encourage kids to eat quinoa, since most children love the flavour of peanut butter. Omit the cilantro, and substitute Wow Butter for the peanut butter if there are any allergies.

NUTRITIONAL INFORMATION PER SERVING

Calories	210
Carbohydrates	24 g
Fibre	3 g
Protein	8 g
Fat	10 g
Saturated Fat	2 g
Cholesterol	0 mg
Sodium	380 mg

1 cup (250 mL) quinoa, rinsed and drained

1½ cups (375 mL) reduced-sodium chicken stock

¾ cup (185 mL) thinly sliced carrots

¾ cup 185 mL) thinly sliced red bell pepper

¼ cup (60 mL) chopped fresh cilantro leaves

⅓ cup (80 mL) sliced green onions

DRESSING

2 Tbsp (30 mL) peanut butter

1½ Tbsp (22 mL) fresh lemon juice

4 tsp (20 mL) reduced-sodium soy sauce

1 Tbsp (15 mL) liquid honey

1½ tsp (7 mL) sesame oil

2 tsp (10 mL) water

⅓ cup (80 mL) chopped toasted cashews or peanuts for garnish (see Tip, page 35)

1. In a saucepan, bring the quinoa and stock to a boil. Cover, reduce the heat to low and simmer for about 15 minutes, until the quinoa is tender and most of the liquid has been absorbed. Transfer to a serving bowl and set aside to cool slightly.

2. Add the carrots, peppers, cilantro and green onions and stir to combine.

3. In a small bowl, whisk together the peanut butter, lemon juice, soy sauce, honey, sesame oil and water until smooth. Pour over the cooled quinoa and toss to combine. Garnish with cashews and serve.

COBB PASTA SALAD

Planning a picnic but tired of the standard fare? Reimagine the classic potato salad with a California twist. This healthy dish includes all the elements of a Cobb salad—including tomatoes, corn, avocado, chicken and cheese—but with the addition of whole-wheat pasta and a delicious simple Russian dressing.

PREP TIME:
11
MINUTES

COOK TIME:
15
MINUTES

MAKES 4 SERVINGS

NUTRITION TIP

There's loads of nutrition in this one-dish meal. The whole-wheat pasta gives you an extra boost of fibre (close to double that of white pasta). Arugula beats iceberg lettuce in nutrition with eight times the calcium, five times the amount of vitamins A, C and K, and four times the iron. Avocado contains folic acid and vitamin B6, which is associated with a lower risk of heart disease.

FOR KIDS

If your kids don't love whole-wheat pasta, try using the smallest pasta shape you can find, such as macaroni. For a milder taste, substitute mozzarella or Havarti for the cheddar cheese.

NUTRITIONAL INFORMATION PER SERVING

Calories	419
Carbohydrates	55 g
Fibre	8 g
Protein	20 g
Fat	12 g
Saturated Fat	5 g
Cholesterol	36 mg
Sodium	269 mg

PASTA SALAD

8 oz (230 g) dried whole-wheat rotini pasta

1½ cups (375 mL) lightly packed arugula or baby spinach leaves

1 cup (250 mL) corn niblets (canned or frozen; if canned, rinsed and drained)

1 cup (250 mL) grape tomatoes

4 oz (120 g) cooked skinless boneless chicken breast, sliced

½ cup (125 mL) sliced avocado (about ¼ avocado)

2 oz (60 g) shredded light white cheddar cheese

DRESSING

2 Tbsp (30 mL) reduced-fat mayonnaise

3 Tbsp (45 mL) reduced-fat sour cream

2 Tbsp (30 mL) ketchup or sweet chili sauce

2 Tbsp (30 mL) water

1. **Make the pasta salad:** In a pot of boiling water, cook the pasta according to the package directions, until just firm to the bite (al dente). Drain well and rinse under cold running water until completely cooled; drain well.

2. Transfer the cooled pasta to a large serving bowl. Add the arugula and toss to combine. Set aside.

3. Heat a small skillet over high heat. Lightly spray the skillet with vegetable oil, then add the corn and tomatoes. Sauté just until the vegetables begin to brown, about 3 minutes. Remove the pan from the heat and set aside.

4. **Make the dressing:** In a small bowl, whisk together the mayonnaise, sour cream, ketchup and water. Pour onto the pasta and toss until well coated.

5. On top of the pasta, arrange the cooked corn and tomatoes, chicken, avocado and shredded cheese in neat rows (á la the classic Cobb). Serve.

PASTA SALAD WITH ROASTED TOMATOES AND ASIAGO CHEESE

This Mediterranean-inspired vegetarian pasta salad can be served as either a main course or side dish. Roasting the tomatoes brings out their natural sweetness, and their juices provide great flavour and reduce the need for excess oil. Breadcrumbs add a crunchy texture and nice contrast to this simple but delicious pasta salad.

PREP TIME:
10
MINUTES

COOK TIME:
15
MINUTES

MAKES 6 SERVINGS

NUTRITION TIP

There are slight differences in red and yellow tomatoes. They contain the same amounts of calories and protein, but red tomatoes deliver more fibre, vitamin C and vitamin A. Yellow tomatoes are higher in iron and zinc and folate. Both are incredibly healthy!

FOR KIDS

Children love the shape and flavour of cherry tomatoes over larger sliced tomatoes, so this dish is perfect for them. Use Parmesan rather than Asiago cheese, as it's milder tasting.

NUTRITIONAL INFORMATION PER SERVING

Calories	250
Carbohydrates	27 g
Fibre	5 g
Protein	13 g
Fat	9 g
Saturated Fat	3.5 g
Cholesterol	15 mg
Sodium	290 mg

¾ cup (185 mL) sliced red cherry tomatoes

¾ cup (185 mL) sliced yellow cherry tomatoes

2 tsp (10 mL) extra virgin olive oil

1 tsp (5 mL) minced garlic

Salt and pepper

¼ cup (60 mL) seasoned dry breadcrumbs or panko

8 oz (230 g) dried whole-wheat penne pasta

¾ cup (185 mL) freshly grated Asiago or Parmesan cheese

¼ cup (60 mL) chopped fresh basil leaves

1. Preheat the oven to 400°F (200°C). Lightly spray a 9-inch (23 cm) baking dish with vegetable oil.

2. Place the tomatoes, oil, garlic, and salt and pepper in the prepared baking dish and toss to combine. Sprinkle with the breadcrumbs.

3. Bake in the preheated oven for about 15 minutes, just until the tomato skins start to crack and lose some of their juices. Remove from the oven.

4. Meanwhile, in a saucepan of boiling water, cook the pasta according to the package instructions, until firm to the bite (al dente). Drain well and transfer to a serving bowl.

5. Add the roasted tomatoes, cheese and basil and gently toss to combine. Serve warm or room temperature.

BLACK BEAN, MANDARIN ORANGE AND BABY SHRIMP SALAD

This salad makes a great starter when served in Boston lettuce leaf cups. If using frozen shrimp, be sure to defrost, drain and dry them completely or the excess liquid will water down the dressing. When mandarin oranges or tangerines are in season, replace the canned fruit with fresh citrus.

PREP TIME:
15
MINUTES

COOK TIME:
3
MINUTES

MAKES 4 SERVINGS   **DAIRY FREE**    **GLUTEN FREE**

NUTRITION TIP

A 6-ounce (175 g) serving of shrimp contains only 200 calories. It's also a high-quality lean protein and low in mercury.

FOR KIDS

If your children don't care for black beans, substitute either white navy beans or chickpeas. Omit the red onion, jalapeños, Dijon and cumin, and substitute chopped fresh parsley for the cilantro.

NUTRITIONAL INFORMATION PER SERVING
(2 LETTUCE CUPS)

Calories	110
Carbohydrates	12 g
Fibre	4 g
Protein	10 g
Fat	3 g
Saturated Fat	0.4 g
Cholesterol	50 mg
Sodium	200 mg

- ½ cup (125 mL) corn niblets (canned or frozen; if canned, rinsed and drained)
- 4 oz (120 g) baby cocktail shrimp
- ½ cup (125 mL) canned mandarin oranges, drained and patted dry
- ½ cup (125 mL) black beans, rinsed and drained
- ½ cup (125 mL) diced red bell pepper
- ¼ cup (60 mL) diced red onion
- 1½ tsp (7 mL) extra virgin olive oil
- 1½ Tbsp (22 mL) fresh lemon juice
- 1 tsp (5 mL) liquid honey
- ½ tsp (2 mL) minced seeded jalapeño pepper
- ½ tsp (2 mL) Dijon mustard
- ¼ tsp (1 mL) ground cumin
- 3 Tbsp (45 mL) chopped fresh cilantro or mint leaves
- Salt and pepper
- 8 Boston lettuce leaves

1. Heat a small skillet over medium-high heat. Lightly spray with vegetable oil, then add the corn. Sauté for 3 minutes, just until lightly charred.

2. In a serving bowl, combine the charred corn, shrimp, oranges, black beans, red pepper, onion, oil, lemon juice, honey, jalapeño, Dijon, cumin, cilantro, and salt and pepper. Toss to combine. Divide evenly among lettuce leaves and serve immediately.

KALE CAESAR SALAD WITH SEARED SCALLOPS

If Popeye were around today he might feel somewhat distressed, since kale is pushing spinach out of the limelight. Baby kale (available in most supermarkets—it even comes pre-washed) replaces the romaine lettuce in this classic salad. To eliminate the high calories of traditional Caesar dressing, I combine olive oil and reduced-fat mayonnaise, which cuts the calories and fat considerably.

PREP TIME:
10
MINUTES

COOK TIME:
6
MINUTES

MAKES 4 SERVINGS  **GLUTEN FREE**

NUTRITION TIP

Kale is a true superfood. It's low in calories and high in fibre, iron, vitamins K and C, and calcium. It's also filled with antioxidants and considered an anti-inflammatory.

FOR KIDS

Substitute spinach or romaine lettuce for the kale if your children haven't yet developed a taste for kale. Try substituting shrimp or grilled chicken for the scallops.

NUTRITIONAL INFORMATION PER SERVING

Calories	270
Carbohydrates	18 g
Fibre	3 g
Protein	18 g
Fat	17 g
Saturated Fat	4 g
Cholesterol	35 mg
Sodium	420 mg

8 cups (2 L) lightly packed baby kale leaves

8 large sea scallops

2 Tbsp + ½ cup (30 mL + 125 mL) freshly grated Parmesan cheese

2 Tbsp (30 mL) reduced-fat mayonnaise

3 Tbsp (45 mL) extra virgin olive oil

3 Tbsp (45 mL) water

2 tsp (10 mL) fresh lemon juice

½ tsp (2 mL) finely chopped garlic

½ tsp (2 mL) Dijon mustard

1. Arrange the kale on a large platter. Set aside.

2. Heat a non-stick skillet over medium-high heat. Lightly spray with vegetable oil, then sauté the scallops for about 3 minutes per side or just until golden brown on the top and bottom and opaque on the sides. (Be careful not to overcook or they will become tough.)

3. In a small bowl, whisk together 2 Tbsp (30 mL) cheese, mayonnaise, olive oil, water, lemon juice, garlic and mustard until smooth. (Alternatively, purée in small food processor.) If the mixture seems too thick, add a little water, a tablespoon at a time, until you reach the desired consistency.

4. Pour the dressing over kale and toss to combine. Sprinkle with the remaining ½ cup (125 mL) cheese and top with the scallops. Serve immediately.

TUNA AND ROASTED POTATO SALAD WITH AVOCADO DRESSING

This unique and delicious salad marries tuna and potato salad and tops them with a creamy, nutrient-rich avocado dressing. It's sure to steal the show at your next lunch or brunch. Roasting the potatoes adds a taste of summer. If you want to really indulge, top the salad with 6 ounces (175 g) of seared fresh tuna, thinly sliced, instead of the canned tuna.

PREP TIME:
15 MINUTES

COOK TIME:
15 MINUTES

MAKES 6 SERVINGS  **GLUTEN FREE**

NUTRITION TIP

Choose light tuna over albacore tuna—light tuna has lower levels of mercury, fewer calories, one-third of the fat and more protein.

FOR KIDS

Avoid serving children albacore tuna, which has higher levels of mercury than light tuna and could be damaging to their nervous system. If desired, you can substitute diced leftover chicken.

NUTRITIONAL INFORMATION PER SERVING

Calories	179
Carbohydrates	24.1 g
Fibre	4.8 g
Protein	13.0 g
Fat	4.2 g
Saturated Fat	1.0 g
Cholesterol	10.7 mg
Sodium	158 mg

12 oz (340 g) baby red potatoes, quartered
2 tsp (10 mL) extra virgin olive oil
¼ tsp (1 mL) chili powder
¼ tsp (1 mL) garlic powder
1 cup (250 mL) corn niblets (canned or frozen; if canned, rinsed and drained)
1 firm avocado, halved, pitted, peeled and diced
¾ cup (185 mL) plain 1% yogurt or reduced-fat sour cream
½ cup (125 mL) packed fresh basil leaves
2 Tbsp (30 mL) fresh lemon juice
1 tsp (5 mL) Sriracha or your favourite hot sauce
Salt and pepper
1 large head romaine lettuce, chopped
1 red bell pepper, seeded and diced
1 can (6 oz/178 g) flaked light or white tuna in water, drained

1. Preheat the oven to 450°F (230°C). Line a baking sheet with foil and lightly spray with vegetable oil.

2. In a bowl, combine the potatoes, oil, and chili and garlic powders and toss until potatoes are well coated. Arrange in a single layer on the prepared baking sheet. Roast in the preheated oven for 15 to 20 minutes or just until tender. Remove from heat and set aside.

3. Meanwhile, in a small skillet lightly sprayed with vegetable oil, sauté the corn for 5 minutes or just until lightly browned. Remove from heat and set aside.

4. In the bowl of a small food processor, combine half of the avocado with the yogurt, basil, lemon juice, Sriracha, and salt and pepper. Purée until smooth. If the mixture seems too thick, add a little water, a tablespoon at a time, until you reach the desired consistency.

5. Arrange the lettuce, red pepper, sautéed corn and roasted potatoes on a serving plate. Pour over the avocado dressing and toss to combine. Top with the tuna and remaining avocado. Serve immediately.

SOUPS

SOUP HAS ALWAYS been the ultimate comfort food. These days a hearty soup full of vegetables, meat, poultry, fish or beans is often a meal in itself. The soups in this chapter reflect the rich cultural diversity in our country; you'll find the flavours of Asia, Africa, and Western Europe, to name just a few.

There's no denying that a homemade stock can be superior in flavour, but making your own on a regular basis can be time-consuming. For ease, I like to use the Tetra packs of either chicken, beef or vegetable stock. Choose brands that are lower in sodium and contain no MSG. Avoid powdered stock bases or bouillon cubes, which are high in sodium.

Use herbs and spices for flavor. Dried herbs can be added during cooking, whereas fresh herbs are more delicate and should be added just before serving.

When making soup, be sure to cover it with a lid and cook over a medium-low heat, stirring occasionally, to ensure the vegetables are cooked evenly and the stock doesn't reduce too much. You can puree your soup in a blender in batches or alternatively, use an immersion blender.

Soups tend to thicken over time; simply add more stock to reach your desired consistency.

My children's number-one soup pick is Fresh Tomato Soup with Grilled Cheese Croutons (page 54)—it's a complete meal in a bowl! Minestrone with Kale, Prosciutto and Cannellini Beans (page 64) has a Mediterranean twist. For a North American flavour, try Baked Smashed Potato Soup with Cheddar (page 59).

FRESH CORN SOUP

This is a fantastic soup to make when fresh corn is in season (it doesn't matter if the corn is yellow, white or bi-coloured). It has a creamy texture, despite containing no cream or butter, and an intense corn flavour. My secret ingredient is evaporated milk! Here's a tip: When picked, fresh corn should squirt a whitish juice. If making this dish out of season, you can use canned peaches and cream corn niblets.

MAKES 6 SERVINGS  **GLUTEN FREE**

NUTRITION TIP

Cooking corn actually increases its nutrition by activating the antioxidants that protect the body from cancer and heart disease. Corn also contains the same amount of calories as an apple and less than one-fourth the sugar.

FOR KIDS

Get children used to eating freshly steamed or grilled corn on the cob without the addition of salt or butter. You can always sprinkle a little grated Parmesan cheese or olive oil over top, which is healthier.

NUTRITIONAL INFORMATION PER SERVING

Calories	140
Carbohydrates	22 g
Fibre	3 g
Protein	7 g
Fat	4 g
Saturated Fat	1 g
Cholesterol	10 mg
Sodium	140 mg

2 tsp (10 mL) vegetable oil
1 ½ cups (375 mL) diced sweet onion
1 ½ tsp (7 mL) minced garlic
6 fresh corn cobs or 6 cups (1.5 L) canned and drained corn niblets
2 cups (500 mL) reduced-sodium chicken or vegetable stock
¼ cup (60 mL) 2% evaporated milk
Salt and pepper
⅓ cup (80 mL) frozen green peas, defrosted and slightly mashed
6 cooked baby cocktail shrimp (optional)

1. In a soup pot over medium heat, heat the oil. Add the onion and garlic, and sauté just until soft, about 5 minutes.

2. Meanwhile, using a sharp knife, cut the kernels from the corn. Add all but ½ cup (125 mL) of the corn kernels (reserve for next step) to the onion mixture and cook for another 3 minutes, until slightly browned.

3. Add the stock, cover, reduce the heat to low and simmer for 5 minutes to let the flavours meld.

4. Transfer the mixture to a food processor. Add the milk and season with salt and pepper. Purée until smooth (hold the lid down with a towel to prevent hot liquid from leaking).

5. Return the mixture to the soup pot, add the remaining ½ cup (125 mL) corn niblets and cook over low heat for about 2 minutes or just until the corn is cooked through.

6. To serve, ladle into soup bowls and garnish with peas and shrimp (if using).

ASPARAGUS SOUP WITH PARMESAN

Asparagus soup is often made creamy by the addition of butter or cream. I like to thicken this soup using potatoes and a small amount of evaporated milk, which gives a creamy texture but is low in calories and fat. I also like to use leeks rather than onions, as they have a milder, sweeter taste. Use only the white part of the leek (reserve the green part to use as a garnish or to make a different soup).

PREP TIME:
10
MINUTES

COOK TIME:
25
MINUTES

MAKES 6 SERVINGS  GLUTEN FREE VEGETARIAN

NUTRITION TIP
Leeks contain more calcium and bone-strengthening manganese than onions. They also contain beta-carotene and vitamin K, which are not present in onions.

FOR KIDS
Since this soup is puréed, your children should like the mild, sweet flavour of the asparagus. If desired, you could substitute 1 small head of broccoli for the asparagus.

NUTRITIONAL INFORMATION PER SERVING

Calories	130
Carbohydrates	20.4 g
Fibre	3.6 g
Protein	5.7 g
Fat	3.1 g
Saturated Fat	0.6 g
Cholesterol	6.3 mg
Sodium	215 mg

2 tsp (10 mL) vegetable oil
2 medium leeks (white part only), thinly sliced, or 1 ½ cups (375 mL) chopped onion
2 tsp (10 mL) minced garlic
½ tsp (2 mL) dried thyme
Salt and pepper
1 ½ cups (375 mL) diced peeled potato
3 cups (750 mL) reduced-sodium vegetable or chicken stock
1 ½ lb (750 g) asparagus, cut into 1-inch (2.5 cm) pieces
⅓ cup (80 mL) 2% evaporated milk
¼ cup (60 mL) freshly grated Parmesan cheese

1. In a soup pot over medium-high heat, heat the oil. Add the leeks, garlic and thyme and sauté for about 5 minutes, until leeks soften. Add the salt, pepper, potato and stock and simmer for about 10 minutes, until the potato is tender. Add the asparagus, reserving the tips. Cook for about 5 minutes, just until the asparagus is tender.

2. Working in batches, transfer the soup to a food processor and purée until smooth (hold the lid down with a towel to prevent hot liquid from leaking).

3. Return the soup to the pot and stir in the milk and cheese. Cook over low heat until heated through, 1 to 2 minutes. Add more stock if the soup seems too thick. Meanwhile, in a small saucepan of boiling water, cook the asparagus tips just until tender, about 2 minutes. Drain in a colander and rinse under cold running water to stop the cooking. Add to the soup and serve.

FRESH TOMATO SOUP WITH GRILLED CHEESE CROUTONS

Tomato soup and grilled cheese sandwiches are a classic combination. In this recipe, I bring the pair even closer by serving tomato soup with grilled cheese croutons! It's interesting, unique and, most importantly, delicious. Be sure to use fresh plum tomatoes to make this soup—they are tastier than canned tomatoes.

PREP TIME:
10
MINUTES

COOK TIME:
20
MINUTES

MAKES 4 SERVINGS  **VEGETARIAN**

NUTRITION TIP

Tomatoes contain a beneficial antioxidant called lycopene, which may lower the risk of heart disease, macular degeneration, bad (LDL) cholesterol and certain cancers such as prostate, lung and stomach.

FOR KIDS

This meal is a real winner with kids.

NUTRITIONAL INFORMATION PER SERVING

Calories	228
Carbohydrates	26.7 g
Fibre	3.3 g
Protein	9.5 g
Fat	9.5 g
Saturated Fat	4.4 g
Cholesterol	18.8 mg
Sodium	521 mg

2 tsp (10 mL) vegetable oil
¾ cup (185 mL) chopped sweet onions (such as Vidalia)
1½ tsp (7 mL) minced garlic
4 cups (1 L) chopped plum tomatoes (about 8), with juices
1 cup (250 mL) reduced-sodium vegetable or chicken stock
1½ Tbsp (22 mL) tomato paste
2 tsp (10 mL) granulated sugar
¼ tsp (1 mL) salt
¼ tsp (1 mL) black pepper
¼ cup (60 mL) chopped fresh basil leaves, for garnish
1 batch Grilled Cheese Croutons (recipe follows)

1. In a non-stick saucepan lightly sprayed with cooking spray, heat the oil over medium heat. Add the onions and garlic and cook for 3 minutes, until the onions are softened. Stir in the tomatoes, stock, tomato paste, sugar, salt and pepper. Bring to a boil. Cover, reduce the heat to low and simmer for 15 minutes.

2. Working in batches, purée soup in a blender or food processor until smooth (hold the lid down with a towel to prevent hot liquid from leaking).

3. Ladle the soup into serving bowls and garnish with the basil. Top each bowl with 2 grilled cheese croutons. Serve immediately.

RECIPE CONTINUED ON NEXT PAGE

FRESH TOMATO SOUP WITH GRILLED CHEESE CROUTONS CONTINUED

GRILLED CHEESE CROUTONS

These cheesy croutons are sure to be a hit with kids and adults alike!

MAKES ABOUT 2 CUPS (500 ML)

2 oz (60 g) shredded light cheddar cheese
2 slices whole-wheat bread

1. While soup is cooking, sprinkle 1 slice of bread evenly with the cheese. Sandwich with the remaining slice of bread.

2. Heat a skillet over medium-high heat. Lightly spray both sides of bread with vegetable oil and cook in hot skillet for 2 minutes per side, just until the cheese melts and the bread is lightly browned.

3. Cut the sandwich into 8 squares. Serve.

PARSNIP SOUP WITH PROSCIUTTO CRISPS

Parsnips are no longer relegated to Sunday roast dinners. They've made a real comeback, along with other trendy root vegetables such as turnips, beets and rutabagas. And why not? Raw parsnips smell like fresh parsley and have an earthy, nutty flavour; cooking brings out their natural sweetness (interestingly, parsnips contain more starch than carrots, which helps thicken this soup naturally).

PREP TIME:

10

MINUTES

COOK TIME:

20

MINUTES

MAKES 6 SERVINGS  **GLUTEN FREE**

NUTRITION TIP

Just ½ cup (125 mL) of cooked sliced parsnips contains 3 grams of fibre and only 55 calories. Parsnips are a good source of vitamin C, folate and manganese, which helps bone formation and to control blood sugar.

FOR KIDS

Kids usually enjoy the sweetness of this root vegetable. Try serving parsnips on their own: cut into chunks (be sure to cut away the tough inner core), drizzle with a little maple syrup and olive oil, and roast in a preheated 400°F (200°C) oven just until tender.

NUTRITIONAL INFORMATION PER SERVING

Calories	148
Carbohydrates	23.4 g
Fibre	3.6 g
Protein	5.5 g
Fat	3.4 g
Saturated Fat	0.6 g
Cholesterol	11.8 mg
Sodium	366 mg

2 tsp (10 mL) vegetable oil
1 leek, white part only, sliced into thin rounds
1½ tsp (7 mL) minced garlic
3 cups (750 mL) cubed peeled parsnips
1 cup (250 mL) diced peeled potato
3½ cups (875 mL) reduced-sodium vegetable or chicken stock
1 tsp (5 mL) Dijon mustard
Salt and pepper
2 oz (60 g) prosciutto, fat trimmed, diced
½ cup (125 mL) 2% evaporated milk

1. In a soup pot over medium-high heat, heat the oil. Add the leek and garlic and sauté for about 5 minutes, until softened. Add the parsnips, potato, stock, Dijon, and salt and pepper. Bring to a boil, then cover, reduce the heat to low and simmer for about 15 minutes, just until the vegetables are soft.

2. Meanwhile, heat a small skillet over medium-high heat. Add the prosciutto and sauté for about 3 minutes, just until crisp. Remove from heat and set aside.

3. Working in batches, transfer the leek mixture to a food processor and process until smooth. Return to the soup pot over low heat and add the milk.

4. Ladle into soup bowls and garnish with the crispy prosciutto. Serve.

BAKED SMASHED POTATO SOUP WITH CHEDDAR

I love baked potatoes, so I decided to turn this favourite side dish into a soup. With its velvety texture, cheesy flavour and crusty baked potato garnish, you're sure to agree that this soup is comfort food.

PREP TIME:
15 MINUTES

COOK TIME:
25 MINUTES

MAKES 6 SERVINGS    GLUTEN FREE   VEGETARIAN

NUTRITION TIP

Yukon gold potatoes are the cream of the crop in terms of flavour and texture—not to mention that one Yukon potato contains half of your daily vitamin C and is a good source of potassium, which can lower blood pressure.

FOR KIDS

Potatoes are one of the best sources of natural starch, which supplies complex carbohydrates for energy—something kids need a lot of.

NUTRITIONAL INFORMATION PER SERVING

Calories	260
Carbohydrates	33.3 g
Fibre	2.2 g
Protein	13.9 g
Fat	8.9 g
Saturated Fat	3.9 g
Cholestero	180 mg
Sodium	314 mg

1 tsp (5 mL) vegetable oil
1 tsp (5 mL) minced garlic
1 cup (250 mL) chopped onion
4 Yukon gold potatoes (about 2 to 2 ½ lb/1 to 1.25 kg), divided
3 cups (750 mL) reduced-sodium vegetable or chicken stock
1 Tbsp (15 ml) olive oil
6 Tbsp (90 mL) freshly grated Parmesan cheese, divided
Salt and pepper
1 cup (250 mL) shredded sharp (old) cheddar cheese, divided
¼ tsp (1 mL) black pepper
¼ cup (60 mL) diced green onions
¼ cup (60 mL) reduced-fat sour cream

1. Preheat the oven to 450°F (230°F). Lightly spray a baking sheet with vegetable oil.

2. In a soup pot over medium-high heat, heat the oil. Add the garlic and onion and sauté for about 3 minutes, just until softened.

3. Peel 3 of the potatoes and dice (do not peel the remaining potato; reserve for the next step). Add to the saucepan along with the stock. Bring to a boil, then cover, reduce the heat to low and simmer until the potatoes are tender, about 20 minutes.

4. Cut the remaining potato (unpeeled) into 12 chunks. Place in a small saucepan of boiling water and cook for about 5 minutes, just until tender. Drain well and transfer to a bowl. Add olive oil, 2 Tbsp of the Parmesan, and the salt and pepper, and toss to coat well. Arrange in a single layer on the prepared baking sheet and roast in the preheated oven for 15 minutes, until lightly browned. Remove from the oven and mash gently with a fork.

RECIPE CONTINUED ON NEXT PAGE

BAKED SMASHED POTATO SOUP WITH CHEDDAR CONTINUED

5. Working in batches, transfer the soup to a food processor or blender and purée until smooth. Return the puréed soup to the saucepan. Stir in ¾ cup (185 mL) of the cheddar and the remaining Parmesan. Simmer, stirring constantly, for about 2 minutes or until the cheese is completely melted.

6. Ladle into soup bowls and garnish each with a spoonful of the roasted mashed potato, black pepper, green onions, sour cream and the remaining cheddar. Serve.

KALE AND YUKON GOLD POTATO SOUP

While this dish may look like asparagus or broccoli soup, the star ingredient is kale. Curly kale is the most common variety of kale sold in bunches at supermarkets. It has tight ruffled dark green or purple leaves that can be difficult to chop, but easy to tear if fresh. It has a noticeable pungent flavour with peppery and bitter tones, so seek out younger-looking leaves—they are somewhat less bitter.

PREP TIME:
15
MINUTES

COOK TIME:
25
MINUTES

MAKES 6 SERVINGS GLUTEN FREE  VEGETARIAN

NUTRITION TIP

Kale is truly a super vegetable. Each cup (250 mL) contains only 40 calories, 3 grams of protein and close to 3 grams of fibre. It improves the blood sugar levels of type 2 diabetics; it also contains potassium, which reduces blood pressure levels.

FOR KIDS

If your kids don't like the large curly kale leaves, try serving them baby kale leaves, which taste more like spinach.

NUTRITIONAL INFORMATION PER SERVING

Calories	176
Carbohydrates	28 g
Fibre	3.3 g
Protein	8.8 g
Fat	3.9 g
Saturated Fat	1.0 g
Cholesterol	3.2 mg
Sodium	196 mg

2 tsp (10 mL) vegetable oil
1½ cups (375 mL) diced onions
2 tsp (10 mL) chopped garlic
3 cups (750 mL) diced peeled Yukon gold potatoes
4 cups (1 L) reduced-sodium vegetable or chicken stock
6 cups (1.5 L) lightly packed chopped kale leaves

1 tsp (5 mL) Worcestershire sauce
Salt and pepper

GARNISH
¼ cup (60 mL) freshly grated Parmesan cheese
2 Tbsp (30 mL) plain 1% yogurt

1. In large soup pot over medium-high heat, heat the oil. Add the onions and garlic and sauté for about 5 minutes, just until softened. Add the potatoes and stock. Cover and simmer for 10 to 15 minutes, just until the potatoes are tender.

2. Stir in the kale, Worcestershire, and salt and pepper. Cover, reduce the heat to low, and simmer for another 5 minutes or just until the kale has wilted.

3. Working in batches, transfer the soup to a food processor and purée until smooth (hold the lid down with a towel to prevent hot liquid from leaking). Return to the soup pot and reheat if necessary.

4. Ladle into soup bowls and garnish with the Parmesan and a dollop of yogurt. Serve.

SWEET POTATO PEANUT SOUP

In West Africa, the combination of sweet potatoes and peanuts is common in many dishes. In this thick and creamy soup, the peanut flavour is balanced by the earthy sweetness of sweet potatoes. It's so filling, a small bowl is all you need. I have lightened it up by using light coconut milk and tomato juice. Be sure to use natural peanut butter to avoid added sugars or hydrogenated oils.

PREP TIME:
15 MINUTES

COOK TIME:
22 MINUTES

MAKES 6 SERVINGS **DAIRY FREE** **GLUTEN FREE**  **VEGETARIAN**

NUTRITION TIP

Peanut butter can be high in calories and fat, but it is a heart-healthy fat, which can increase your good (HDL) cholesterol. It also contains fibre and protein that fill you up and keep you full for longer, so you eat less.

FOR KIDS

If your kids like peanut butter, this soup is a real winner. If there is a peanut allergy, substitute an equal amount of almond or seed butter for the peanut butter. If desired, you can omit the Sriracha and cilantro.

NUTRITIONAL INFORMATION PER SERVING

Calories	242
Carbohydrates	23 g
Fibre	0.1 g
Protein	9.6 g
Fat	12.8 g
Saturated Fat	2.4 g
Cholesterol	3.2 mg
Sodium	275 mg

1 tsp (5 mL) vegetable oil
1 cup (250 mL) chopped onions
1½ tsp (7 mL) minced garlic
2 tsp (10 mL) grated peeled fresh ginger
3 cups (750 mL) reduced-sodium vegetable stock
1½ cups (375 mL) diced peeled sweet potatoes
¾ cup (185 mL) diced carrots
1 cup (250 mL) tomato juice
½ cup (125 mL) smooth peanut butter

1 tsp (5 mL) granulated sugar (optional)
1 tsp (5 mL) Sriracha or your favourite hot sauce
1 cup (250 mL) light coconut milk

GARNISH

3 Tbsp (45 mL) chopped unsalted roasted peanuts
⅓ cup (80 mL) chopped seeded tomatoes
2 Tbsp (30 mL) chopped fresh cilantro leaves

1. In a soup pot over medium-high heat, heat the oil. Add the onions, garlic and ginger and sauté for about 3 minutes, until onions are soft. Stir in the stock, sweet potatoes and carrots. Cover, reduce the heat to low and simmer for 15 minutes or just until the vegetables are tender.

2. Working in batches, transfer the soup to a food processor along with the tomato juice, peanut butter, sugar (if using) and Sriracha and purée until smooth (hold the lid down with a towel to prevent hot liquid from leaking). Return the mixture to the soup pot. Add coconut milk.

3. Ladle into soup bowls and garnish with the peanuts, tomatoes and cilantro. Serve.

MISO SOUP WITH SOBA NOODLES AND CHICKEN

Miso soup is a traditional Japanese soup. The stock is made from dashi, a type of kelp, and miso paste, which is made from fermented soybeans. (I like to use white miso, which has a milder flavour than other varieties.) To simplify things, I replace the dashi with chicken stock. This soup is very versatile: If desired, substitute firm tofu or shrimp for the chicken.

MAKES 6 SERVINGS **DAIRY FREE**

NUTRITION TIP

Miso paste is a complete protein, which means it contains nine of the essential amino acids necessary for the dietary needs of our bodies. This makes it perfect for vegetarians or vegans. It is also a good vegetable source of B vitamins, especially B12.

FOR KIDS

If your child doesn't like the flavour of miso paste, you can reduce the amount by half or even substitute an equal amount of peanut butter or tahini.

NUTRITIONAL INFORMATION PER SERVING

Calories	118
Carbohydrates	16.2 g
Fibre	1.0 g
Protein	11.7 g
Fat	1.7 g
Saturated Fat	0.5 g
Cholesterol	10.4 mg
Sodium	373 mg

3 oz (90 g) dried soba noodles or whole-wheat spaghetti pasta

4 oz (120 g) boneless skinless chicken breast, pounded flat

5 cups (1.25 L) reduced-sodium chicken stock

2 Tbsp (30 mL) white miso paste

1 Tbsp (15 mL) reduced-sodium soy sauce

1 tsp (5 mL) minced peeled fresh ginger

3 Tbsp (45 mL) chopped green onions, for garnish

2 Tbsp (30 mL) chopped fresh cilantro or flat-leaf parsley leaves, for garnish

1. Bring a pot of water to a boil. Cook the noodles according to the package instructions, just until tender. Drain well.

2. Meanwhile, in a skillet or grill pan lightly sprayed with vegetable oil, cook the chicken until no longer pink inside, about 5 minutes. Set aside for a few minutes to rest, then cut into ½-inch (1 cm) pieces.

3. In a large saucepan over medium heat, bring the chicken stock to a boil. Stir in the miso, soy sauce and ginger. Cover, reduce the heat to medium-low and simmer for 5 minutes to let the flavours meld. Stir in the cooked noodles and chicken pieces.

4. Ladle the soup into small bowls and garnish with green onions and cilantro. Serve.

MINESTRONE WITH KALE, PROSCIUTTO AND CANNELLINI BEANS

Minestrone, a soup of Italian origin, is traditionally a thick soup made with vegetables and either pasta, rice or beans. Since kale is such a nutritional powerhouse, I decided to add it to this tasty soup along with white kidney beans. If you don't care for the taste of regular kale, try baby kale instead, which is softer and sweeter. Prosciutto adds a buttery, sweet and slightly salty flavour to the soup.

PREP TIME:
15 MINUTES

COOK TIME:
25 MINUTES

MAKES 6 SERVINGS  **GLUTEN FREE**

NUTRITION TIP

One cup (250 mL) of kale contains only 33 calories, 3 grams of protein, 2.5 grams of fibre and folate, a B vitamin that's key for brain development and essential to prenatal development.

FOR KIDS

Make this soup using baby kale or baby spinach, which is softer and sweeter than regular kale.

NUTRITIONAL INFORMATION PER SERVING

Calories	209
Carbohydrates	30.3 g
Fibre	8.5 g
Protein	13.2 g
Fat	4.9 g
Saturated Fat	1.3 g
Cholesterol	11.4 mg
Sodium	597 mg

2 tsp (10 mL) vegetable oil
1 cup (250 mL) diced onion
1 cup (250 mL) diced carrot
2 oz (60 g) diced prosciutto, fat trimmed
2 tsp (10 mL) minced garlic
4 cups (1 L) reduced-sodium chicken stock
1 can (28 oz/828 mL) diced tomatoes, with juice
1 can (15 oz/444 mL) cannellini (white kidney) beans, rinsed and drained
2 cups (500 mL) lightly packed sliced kale leaves
1 cup (250 mL) diced peeled Yukon gold potato
1 tsp (5 mL) dried basil
¼ cup (60 mL) freshly grated Parmesan cheese
Chopped fresh flat-leaf parsley leaves, for garnish
Additional Parmesan cheese, for finishing (optional)

1. In a large saucepan over medium-high heat, heat the oil. Add the onion and carrot and sauté for 5 minutes, just until the carrot is tender. Add the prosciutto and garlic and sauté for another 5 minutes or until the prosciutto begins to brown.

2. Stir in the stock, tomatoes, beans, kale, potato and basil. Cover, reduce the heat to low and simmer for 15 minutes or just until the potatoes are tender. Add the Parmesan.

3. Ladle into soup bowls and garnish with parsley and additional Parmesan, if desired.

CURRIED CHICKEN SOUP

This is such a simple yet delicious soup. Curry has a unique flavour due to the combination of both savoury and sweet spices.

PREP TIME:
10
MINUTES

COOK TIME:
20
MINUTES

MAKES 6 SERVINGS **DAIRY FREE** **GLUTEN FREE**

NUTRITION TIP

Store-bought chicken stock can contain over 800 mg of sodium per cup (250 mL). Look for reduced-sodium varieties, which should only contain about 150 mg sodium. Even better: Make your own stock and add fresh herbs such as basil, parsley or thyme, and just a small amount of sea salt.

FOR KIDS

Chicken soup is soul food for children—it makes them feel better no matter what! Omit the curry if your kids aren't fans of the flavour.

6 cups (1.5 L) reduced-sodium chicken stock, divided
1 large bone-in skin-on chicken breast (about 1 lb/500 g)
1 cup (250 mL) diced carrots

2 tsp (10 mL) vegetable oil
1½ cups (375 mL) diced onion
1 tsp (5 mL) minced garlic
1½ tsp (7 mL) curry powder
⅓ cup (80 mL) white rice

1. In large saucepan over high heat, combine 3 cups (750 mL) of the chicken stock, the chicken breast and the carrots. Bring to a boil, then cover, reduce the heat to low, and simmer for 10 to 12 minutes or just until chicken is cooked through. Using a slotted spoon, transfer the cooked chicken and carrots to a bowl and set aside to cool slightly. Reserve the broth in the pan. Once cooled slightly, dice the reserved chicken; set aside with the carrots.

2. Meanwhile, in another saucepan over medium-high heat, heat the oil. Add the onion, garlic and curry powder and sauté for 5 minutes or just until the onions are soft. Stir in the remaining 3 cups (750 mL) of stock and the rice. Cover, bring to a boil and then reduce the heat to medium and simmer for 10 minutes or until the rice is tender.

3. Using a food processor, purée mixture until smooth (hold the lid down with a towel to prevent hot liquid from leaking). (Alternatively, use a stand blender.) Add just enough of the reserved broth to thin soup to desired consistency (reserve the remaining broth for another use). Stir in the reserved carrots and diced chicken, and cook just until heated through.

4. Ladle into soup bowls and serve.

NUTRITIONAL INFORMATION PER SERVING

Calories	187
Carbohydrates	17.9 g
Fibre	1.5 g
Protein	18.7 g
Fat	4.7 g
Saturated Fat	1.0 g
Cholesterol	33.8 mg
Sodium	118 mg

USING RICE TO THICKEN SOUP

There are many ways to thicken a soup—by adding flour, cornstarch, butter or cream—but I discovered that overcooking short- or medium-grain rice in broth and then puréeing it using an immersion blender not only thickens soup (thanks to the starch in the rice), but adds a velvety texture and creamy taste similar to butter or cream without the calories and fat.

CREAMY SALMON CHOWDER

Fish chowder is a one-pot meal. Thickened with flour and lower-fat milk, this chowder combines hearty vegetables and fresh salmon. The key is not to overcook the salmon so it remains moist. (You can also use canned salmon, drained and with the bones removed.) If you don't like salmon, substitute another firm-fleshed fish such as tilapia, halibut, swordfish or grouper.

PREP TIME:
20
MINUTES

COOK TIME:
25
MINUTES

MAKES 6 SERVINGS

NUTRITION TIP

Salmon is an excellent source of omega-3 fatty acids that help reduce the risk of cardiovascular disease. To avoid excess mercury, avoid farmed Atlantic salmon; instead purchase organic or wild Pacific salmon.

FOR KIDS

If the taste of salmon is too strong for your kids, try making this chowder with a mild fish, such as tilapia or lake trout.

NUTRITIONAL INFORMATION PER SERVING

Calories	225
Carbohydrates	25.3 g
Fibre	2.5 g
Protein	12.5 g
Fat	7.5 g
Saturated Fat	1.8 g
Cholesterol	28.4 mg
Sodium	253.4 mg

2 slices diced prosciutto (about 1 oz/30 g; optional)

2 tsp (10 mL) vegetable oil

1 cup (250 mL) diced onion

1½ tsp (7 mL) minced garlic

1 can (11½ oz/341 mL) corn niblets, rinsed and drained

½ cup (125 mL) diced carrots

1½ cups (375 mL) diced peeled potato

3 cups (750 mL) reduced-sodium vegetable or chicken stock

3 Tbsp (45 mL) all-purpose flour

2 cups (500 mL) 2% milk

8 oz (230 g) salmon fillet (skinless), diced

Salt and pepper

3 Tbsp (45 mL) chopped fresh dill, for garnish

1. Heat a small skillet over medium-high heat. Add the prosciutto and sauté for 2 minutes or just until crisp. Remove from the heat and set aside.

2. In large soup pot, heat the oil. Add the onion and sauté for 5 minutes, until softened. Stir in the garlic and corn, and sauté for about 3 minutes or until corn starts to brown. Stir in the carrots, potato and stock. Cover, reduce the heat to low and simmer for about 15 minutes, until the potato is tender.

3. Transfer 2 cups (500 mL) of the mixture to a food processor and purée until smooth (hold the lid down with a towel to prevent hot liquid from leaking). Return to the pot.

4. In a small bowl, combine the flour and milk and stir until smooth. Add to the soup and simmer just until slightly thickened, about 3 minutes. Add the salmon and salt and pepper, and simmer for another 2 minutes, just until the salmon is opaque and cooked through.

5. Ladle into soup bowls and garnish with the dill and reserved crispy prosciutto. Serve.

VEGETABLES

VEGETABLES ARE ONE of the healthiest foods you can consume, and you should eat 7 to 8 servings of vegetables per day. Eating a diet rich in veggies may lower the risk of cancers, heart disease, high blood pressure, high cholesterol and intestinal disorders, and can help prevent obesity. Vegetables contain the lowest amount of calories, fat and sodium compared with other food groups. Leaving the skin on vegetables, if it's not discoloured or bruised, increases their fibre content. I like to think of vegetables as "nature's candy."

If you'd like to cook vegetables ahead of time to cut down on prep before dinner, they can be steamed, blanched, boiled or microwaved. Cook vegetables just until tender crisp to retain their colour and texture. Drain and rinse under cold running water to prevent overcooking.

You can always substitute frozen vegetables for fresh, but skip canned vegetables—they are often high in sodium and lack colour and texture.

When sautéing vegetables, use a skillet lightly sprayed with vegetable oil, and stick to the amount of fat specified in the recipe. If the vegetables begin to burn and stick, respray or add a little water to the skillet. Do not add more oil or butter, which is where excess calories and fat creep in.

For a trendy vegetarian dish, try Cauliflower Steak with Sun-dried Tomato and Olives (page 80) or Portobello Pizza (page 76). Pesto Smashed Potatoes (page 73) are a family favourite. Kids will also love Sloppy Joe Baked Potatoes (page 75).

ROASTED BRUSSELS SPROUT SALAD WITH APRICOTS AND TOASTED ALMONDS

Traditionally, Brussels sprouts are boiled and served as a side dish, which many people do not love. In this tasty salad, I roast them and pair them with sweet apricots and orange juice, which nicely balances the stronger flavour of the sprouts.

PREP TIME:
10 MINUTES

COOK TIME:
15 MINUTES

MAKES 6 SERVINGS DAIRY FREE  GLUTEN FREE  VEGETARIAN

NUTRITION TIP

These tiny cabbages are high in fibre, which lowers bad (LDL) cholesterol to improve heart health. Brussels sprouts contain phytonutrients that can kill cancer cells.

FOR KIDS

Kids usually don't like boiled Brussels sprouts, but you may win the battle by roasting them, then slicing them thinly. If not, try roasting broccoli and cutting it into small pieces.

NUTRITIONAL INFORMATION PER SERVING

Calories	169
Carbohydrates	20.8 g
Fibre	6.6 g
Protein	5.8 g
Fat	8.2 g
Saturated Fat	0.9 g
Cholesterol	0 mg
Sodium	117 mg

1½ lb (750 g) Brussels sprouts, trimmed and quartered

1 tsp (5 mL) freshly grated orange zest

3 Tbsp (45 mL) orange juice

2 Tbsp (30 mL) extra virgin olive oil

2 tsp (10 mL) Dijon mustard

½ tsp (2 mL) minced garlic

Salt and pepper

10 dried apricots, thinly sliced

⅓ cup (80 mL) sliced blanched almonds, toasted (see Tip, page 35)

1. Preheat the oven to 425°F (220°C). Lightly spray a baking sheet with vegetable oil.

2. Place the Brussels sprouts on the prepared baking sheet, spray lightly with vegetable oil and roast in the preheated oven for 15 minutes or just until tender and browned.

3. Meanwhile, in a bowl, whisk together the orange zest and juice, oil, mustard, garlic, and salt and pepper.

4. Transfer the roasted Brussels sprouts to a serving dish. Drizzle with dressing and toss to combine. Sprinkle with apricots and toasted almonds. Serve.

BAKED POTATO PARMESAN CHIPS

Everyone loves potato chips, but you know you can't stop at just a handful. Try my tasty version of oven-baked chips, which contain a fraction of the calories and fat. The key is to thinly slice the potatoes (use a sharp knife, a mandolin or your food processor fitted with the slicing blade).

MAKES 4 SERVINGS  GLUTEN FREE   VEGETARIAN

NUTRITION TIP

Just 1 oz (30 g) of potato chips, about 15 chips, contains over 160 calories and 10 grams of fat. My baked chips contain about 125 calories and only 3.5 grams of fat!

FOR KIDS

Kids will love these crispy chips. Try to get your kids eating these before they become "addicted" to processed varieties.

NUTRITIONAL INFORMATION PER SERVING

Calories	127
Carbohydrates	20.1 g
Fibre	1.4 g
Protein	2.9 g
Fat	3.6 g
Saturated Fat	0.6 g
Cholesterol	1.1 mg
Sodium	99 mg

1 lb (500 g) Yukon gold potatoes (unpeeled)
1 Tbsp (15 mL) olive oil
Salt and pepper
1 Tbsp (15 mL) freshly grated Parmesan cheese

1. Preheat the oven to 450°F (230°C). Line a baking sheet with foil and lightly spray with vegetable oil.

2. Slice the potatoes crosswise into ⅛-inch (3 mm) thick rounds. Transfer to a large bowl. Add the oil, salt, pepper and cheese and toss until well coated.

3. Arrange the slices in a single layer on the prepared baking sheet, ensuring they are not overlapping. Bake in the preheated oven for 10 minutes. Remove from oven, turn over and rotate the baking sheet, then bake for another 10 minutes, until crisp and lightly browned. Serve immediately.

PESTO SMASHED POTATOES

Yukon Gold potatoes have a thin skin that can be eaten, so you don't need to peel them before making smashed potatoes. The skin is a great source of vitamin C, vitamin B6, copper, potassium, zinc and protein. And a bonus: Their golden flesh gives this dish its distinct buttery flavour and creamy texture, so there's no need to add butter. (Pictured in the background on page 140.)

PREP TIME:
5
MINUTES

COOK TIME:
17
MINUTES

MAKES 4 SERVINGS    GLUTEN FREE   VEGETARIAN

NUTRITION TIP

The Yukon Gold potato contains nearly twice as much vitamin C as a regular baking potato and provides half of your daily need for potassium.

FOR KIDS

Your kids will love this dish. The vitamin C in potatoes helps to strengthen a child's immune system.

NUTRITIONAL INFORMATION PER SERVING

Calories	344
Carbohydrates	44.6 g
Fibre	3.4 g
Protein	9.2 g
Fat	13.9 g
Saturated Fat	2.1 g
Cholesterol	7.9 mg
Sodium	151 mg

2 lb (1 kg) whole Yukon gold potatoes (unpeeled), cut into ½-inch (1 cm) slices
2 Tbsp (30 mL) olive oil
½ cup (125 mL) 2% milk
Salt and pepper
⅓ cup (80 mL) pesto sauce (store-bought or see recipe page 33)
2 Tbsp (30 mL) sliced blanched almonds, toasted (see Tip, page 35)

1. In a large saucepan of boiling water, bring the potatoes to a boil. Reduce the heat and simmer for 15 minutes or just until tender. Drain well and return to the pan over low heat until the potatoes are steamed dry, about 2 minutes. Transfer to a bowl.

2. Using the back of a wooden spoon, smash the cooked potatoes. Add the oil, milk, salt, pepper and pesto, and stir just until combined but still chunky. Sprinkle with almonds and serve.

ROASTED SWEET POTATO SKINS WITH TZATZIKI

Potato skins are so popular that I decided to develop a healthier version using sweet potatoes, as they contain more nutrients. I avoid a long roasting time by microwaving them instead, then finish by roasting them for a few minutes for a crunchy texture. I like to serve this as a side dish to grilled fish or chicken.

MAKES 4 SERVINGS  GLUTEN FREE  VEGETARIAN

NUTRITION TIP

Sweet potato skins contain an abundance of nutrients, have more vitamin C, fewer calories, more fibre and fewer total carbs than white potatoes.

FOR KIDS

Children love the sweetness and bright colour of this healthy vegetable. Sweet potatoes are high in vitamins C and E, which prevent cell damage in young chidren.

NUTRITIONAL INFORMATION PER SERVING (½ POTATO)

Calories	102
Carbohydrates	6.5 g
Fibre	0.9 g
Protein	5.1 g
Fat	6.6 g
Saturated Fat	2.4 g
Cholesterol	10 mg
Sodium	236 mg

2 large sweet potatoes
1 Tbsp (15 mL) olive oil
Salt and pepper
⅛ tsp (0.5 mL) chili powder
1 oz (30 g) shredded light mozzarella cheese

1 oz (30 g) shredded sharp (old) white cheddar cheese
¼ cup (60 mL) tzatziki (store-bought)
1 green onion, thinly sliced

1. Preheat the oven to 450°F (230°C). Line a baking sheet with foil.

2. Pierce the potatoes all over with the tines of a fork and microwave on high for 10 minutes or just until tender. Cut the potatoes in half lengthwise and, using a spoon, scoop out the insides, leaving the skins intact. Reserve the cooked potato for another use.

3. Rub the potato skins all over with the oil and sprinkle with salt and pepper and chili powder.

4. Transfer to the prepared baking sheet and bake in the preheated oven for 15 minutes or just until the skins are crisp.

5. Remove from the oven and divide the cheese equally between the skins. Bake for 1 minute or just until the cheese melts.

6. Serve with a dollop of tzatziki and a sprinkling of green onions.

TIP If you don't have a microwave, roast the sweet potatoes in a preheated 425°F (220°C) oven for about 40 minutes, until tender.

SLOPPY JOE BAKED POTATOES

Sloppy Joes have been around since the 1950s. Traditionally the dish is prepared with ground beef, onions and tomato sauce, and is served on a hamburger bun. I like to step it up a notch by serving it over a baked potato and topping it with an array of tasty garnishes. If you have the time and prefer a crispier skin, bake the potatoes at 450°F (230°C) for about 45 minutes.

PREP TIME:
15 MINUTES

COOK TIME:
15 MINUTES

MAKES 6 SERVINGS  **GLUTEN FREE**

NUTRITION TIP

If sodium is an issue, keep in mind that ½ cup (125 mL) of store-bought tomato sauce can contain 400 mg of sodium. Choose reduced-sodium brands whenever possible.

FOR KIDS

This meal is a winner with kids. It is a complete meal in terms of nutrition. Potatoes contain more nutrients than both rice and pasta.

NUTRITIONAL INFORMATION PER SERVING (1 POTATO)

Calories	428
Carbohydrates	56.6 g
Fibre	6.8 g
Protein	29.3 g
Fat	14.2 g
Saturated Fat	4.7 g
Cholesterol	69 mg
Sodium	273 mg

1 tsp (5 mL) vegetable oil
1 cup (250 mL) finely diced onion
1½ tsp (7 mL) minced garlic
12 oz (340 g) extra-lean ground beef
1 spicy beef sausage (4 oz/120 g), casing removed
2 cups (500 mL) tomato sauce (store-bought or homemade)
½ cup (125 mL) reduced-sodium chicken stock
1½ tsp (7 mL) dried basil
1 tsp (5 mL) chili powder
6 medium baking potatoes

GARNISHES (OPTIONAL)

½ cup (125 mL) shredded light cheddar cheese
⅓ cup (80 mL) diced seeded tomato
¼ cup (60 mL) reduced-fat sour cream

1. In a medium saucepan lightly sprayed with vegetable oil, heat the oil over medium-high heat. Add the onion and garlic, and sauté for 5 minutes or until the onion begins to brown. Add the beef and sausage and cook for 5 minutes or until no longer pink, breaking the meat apart with a wooden spoon.

2. Add the tomato sauce, stock, basil and chili powder. Cover, reduce the heat to low and simmer for 15 minutes, stirring occasionally, until thickened.

3. Meanwhile, pierce the potatoes all over using the tines of a fork. Microwave on high for 8 to 12 minutes, or until tender. (Alternatively, roast in a preheated 425°F (220°C) oven for 1 hour, until tender.)

4. To serve, divide the cooked potatoes among serving plates. Cut the potatoes in half lengthwise and top with Sloppy Joe mixture. Garnish with cheese, tomato and sour cream, if desired.

PORTOBELLO PIZZAS

You have to try this healthy and delicious veggie pizza, in which a Portobello cap serves as the crust. I take the toppings of our favourite pizzas and spread them over a large panko-crusted mushroom cap, then bake them until the cheese is melted. You can easily substitute ground turkey or a soy-based protein for the ground beef. These pizzas makes a great main dish or substantial side dish.

PREP TIME:
15
MINUTES

COOK TIME:
17
MINUTES

MAKES 6 SERVINGS

NUTRITION TIP

One large slice of a meat and vegetable pizza contains 300 calories and 14 grams of fat, compared to this more filling alternative, which comes in at around 220 calories and 9 grams of fat.

FOR KIDS

Children will love the toppings on these mushroom pizzas. If they don't like the size of the mushroom, try using smaller white mushrooms and reducing the cooking time to about 10 minutes.

NUTRITIONAL INFORMATION PER SERVING

Calories	227
Carbohydrates	22 g
Fibre	2.6 g
Protein	13.6 g
Fat	9.8 g
Saturated Fat	3.0 g
Cholesterol	54 mg
Sodium	440 mg

¾ cup (185 mL) unseasoned panko or dry breadcrumbs

4 Tbsp (60 mL) freshly grated Parmesan cheese, divided

1 egg

2 Tbsp (30 mL) 2% milk

6 medium Portobello mushrooms, stems removed

2 tsp (10 mL) vegetable oil

2 tsp (10 mL) minced garlic

½ cup (125 mL) diced seeded green bell pepper

½ cup (125 mL) diced carrots

6 oz (175 g) lean ground beef

1⅓ cups (330 mL) tomato sauce (store-bought or homemade)

½ cup (125 mL) shredded light mozzarella cheese

1. Preheat the oven to 425°F (220°C). Line a baking sheet with foil.

2. Prepare a breading station: In a shallow bowl, combine the panko and 2 Tbsp (30 mL) of the Parmesan. In another shallow bowl, whisk together the egg and milk. Dredge the mushroom caps in the egg mixture, then in the panko mixture, coating both sides.

3. Transfer the coated mushroom caps to the prepared baking sheet and lightly spray with vegetable oil. Bake in the preheated oven for 15 minutes or just until tender and browned.

4. Meanwhile, in a skillet over medium heat, heat the oil. Add the garlic, green pepper and carrots and cook for 10 minutes, stirring occasionally, just until the carrots begin to soften. Add the beef and cook, breaking up with the back of a wooden spoon, for 3 minutes, until no longer pink. Stir in the tomato sauce, cover, reduce the heat and simmer for 5 minutes, until thickened slightly.

5. Divide the stuffing between the mushroom caps, top with the mozzarella and remaining 2 Tbsp (30 mL) of Parmesan, and bake in the preheated oven for 2 minutes or just until the cheese melts. Serve.

MEDITERRANEAN-STUFFED PORTOBELLO MUSHROOMS

Portobello mushrooms are fully grown brown mushrooms. Due to their size, they contain less moisture, which gives them a meaty texture and earthy taste—perfect for enjoying as a delicious vegetarian main course or a side dish. Here I dust them with panko crumbs and dip them in egg to keep them moist. The filling makes these a tasty alternative to traditional Greek salad!

PREP TIME:
15
MINUTES

COOK TIME:
20
MINUTES

MAKES 6 SERVINGS **VEGETARIAN**

NUTRITION TIP

Portobello mushrooms are low in fat and high in fibre. One large mushroom contains only 40 calories and 3 grams of fibre. They are also an excellent source of selenium, which is an antioxidant.

FOR KIDS

Your kids may not enjoy the size of Portobello mushrooms. If desired, substitute button mushrooms. You can also replace the feta with a milder cheese and omit the olives.

NUTRITIONAL INFORMATION PER SERVING

Calories	96
Carbohydrates	3.9 g
Fibre	1.4 g
Protein	3.8 g
Fat	5.8 g
Saturated Fat	1.8 g
Cholesterol	2.8 mg
Sodium	250 mg

¾ cup (185 mL) unseasoned panko or dry breadcrumbs
2 Tbsp (30 mL) freshly grated Parmesan cheese
1 egg
2 Tbsp (30 mL) 2% milk
6 large Portobello mushrooms, stems removed
¾ cup (185 mL) diced seeded tomato
¾ cup (185 mL) diced green bell pepper
¾ cup (185 mL) diced cucumber
2½ oz (75 g) cubed light feta cheese
⅓ cup (80 mL) sliced green onion
3 Tbsp (45 mL) chopped pitted black olives
4 tsp (20 mL) extra virgin olive oil
4 tsp (20 mL) fresh lemon juice
½ tsp (5 mL) minced garlic
½ tsp (5 mL) dried basil

1. Preheat the oven to 425°F (220°C). Line a baking sheet with foil.

2. Prepare a breading station: In a shallow bowl, combine the panko and Parmesan. In another shallow bowl, whisk together the egg and milk.

3. Dip the mushroom caps into the egg mixture, coating both sides, and then into the crumb mixture.

4. Place the coated mushroom caps on the prepared baking sheet and lightly spray with vegetable oil. Bake for 15 minutes, just until tender and browned.

5. Meanwhile, in a bowl, combine the tomato, green pepper, cucumber, feta, onion, olives, olive oil, lemon juice, garlic and basil.

6. To serve, divide the roasted Portobellos among the serving plates. Top with the tomato mixture.

EGGPLANT CAPRESE WITH CHERRY TOMATOES AND FETA

Eggplant has an earthy, meaty quality, which makes it a wonderful vegetarian alternative. The key to keeping it healthy is to avoid deep-frying it. This dish is lightly breaded and baked, and makes a perfect appetizer, side dish or main course. There are a few different varieties of eggplant, including the large oblong deep purple-skinned eggplants, baby eggplants and Japanese eggplants, which are long and thin. For this recipe, I prefer using regular large eggplants for their size, but you can use whatever type of eggplant you prefer.

PREP TIME:
10 MINUTES

COOK TIME:
20 MINUTES

MAKES 8 SERVINGS  **VEGETARIAN**

NUTRITION TIP

Eggplant is an excellent source of fibre, vitamins A, B and C, as well as folate. Baking the eggplant rather than deep-frying it reduces the calories and fat.

FOR KIDS

Lightly breading and baking eggplant is a good way to introduce this vegetable to your children. Substitute mozzarella cheese for the feta, if desired.

NUTRITIONAL INFORMATION PER SERVING (1 SLICE)

Calories	124
Carbohydrates	12 g
Fibre	2.5 g
Protein	4.5 g
Fat	6.5 g
Saturated Fat	1.5 g
Cholesterol	21 mg
Sodium	119.5 mg

1 large eggplant

1 egg

¼ cup (60 mL) 2% milk

1 cup (250 mL) seasoned dry breadcrumbs

2 Tbsp (30 mL) freshly grated Parmesan cheese

1½ cups (375 mL) cherry tomatoes, halved lengthwise

¼ cup (60 mL) toasted pine nuts (see Tip, page 35)

1 oz (30 g) light feta cheese, crumbled

2 tsp (10 mL) olive oil

Salt and pepper

Fresh basil, for garnish

1. Preheat the oven to 425°F (220°C). Line a baking sheet with foil and lightly spray with vegetable oil.

2. Slice the eggplant lengthwise into eight ¼-inch (6 mm) thick pieces.

3. Prepare a breading station: In a shallow bowl, whisk together the egg and milk. On another plate, combine the breadcrumbs and Parmesan. Dip the eggplant in the egg wash, then in the breadcrumb mixture. Transfer to the prepared baking sheet.

4. Bake in the preheated oven for 20 minutes, turning halfway, until lightly browned and fork-tender.

5. In a bowl, combine the tomatoes, pine nuts, feta, olive oil, and salt and pepper.

6. To serve, divide the baked eggplant among the serving plates. Top with tomato mixture and garnish with basil.

CAULIFLOWER STEAK WITH SUN-DRIED TOMATO AND OLIVE SALSA

This dish is inspired by an entrée my daughter, who is a vegetarian, once ordered at a restaurant in Las Vegas. It was so delicious that I had to develop my own version. It's a very elegant way to serve cauliflower, and it works equally well as a first course, side dish or main course. Once you have tasted roasted cauliflower, you'll never want to boil it again!

PREP TIME:
10 MINUTES

COOK TIME:
21 MINUTES

MAKES 8 SERVINGS    **GLUTEN FREE**   **VEGETARIAN**

NUTRITION TIP

Cauliflower is part of the cruciferous family of vegetables, which includes broccoli and Brussels sprouts. One serving (1 cup/250 mL) contains over 77% of your daily vitamin C requirement, which acts as an antioxidant.

FOR KIDS

If your children are apprehensive about cauliflower, roasting it, which brings out its sweet flavour, may change their minds. If desired, you can omit the olives. You can also try serving these "steaks" over a bed of tomato sauce and sprinkle them with shredded mozzarella cheese.

1 large head cauliflower
½ cup (125 mL) thinly sliced pitted black olives
6 sun-dried tomatoes, rehydrated (see Tip, page 14), thinly sliced
2 Tbsp (30 mL) olive oil
½ tsp (5 mL) minced garlic
½ tsp (5 mL) fresh lemon juice
2 Tbsp (30 mL) chopped fresh basil or flat-leaf parsley leaves
1 oz (30 g) light feta cheese, crumbled

1. Preheat the oven to 400°F (200°C). Line a baking sheet with foil.

2. Remove the leaves from the cauliflower, leaving the stem end intact. Cut the entire cauliflower in half crosswise, starting from the top. Then slice each half into four ½-inch (1 cm) to ¾-inch (2 cm) "steaks" (you should end up with 8 pieces; some florets will separate—reserve them for another recipe).

3. Heat a large skillet over medium heat. Lightly spray the skillet with vegetable oil and sauté the cauliflower "steaks" for about 3 minutes per side, just until browned.

4. Transfer the "steaks" to the prepared baking sheet and bake in the preheated oven for 15 to 20 minutes, just until fork-tender.

5. Meanwhile, in a small bowl, combine the olives, tomatoes, olive oil, garlic, lemon juice and basil.

6. To serve, divide the cauliflower steaks among serving plates. Top with the olive mixture and sprinkle the feta over top.

NUTRITIONAL INFORMATION PER SERVING (1 STEAK)

Calories	166
Carbohydrates	14.4 g
Fibre	4.9 g
Protein	6.2 g
Fat	11 g
Saturated Fat	1.7 g
Cholesterol	2.1 mg
Sodium	380 mg

Black Bean Burgers, Kale Parmesan Chips (page 13)

BLACK BEAN BURGERS

I love a delicious veggie burger, but they're often hard to come by. This combination of sautéed mushrooms and black beans with the avocado topping is outstanding. The bun is optional.

PREP TIME:
10 MINUTES

COOK TIME:
18 MINUTES

MAKES 8 SERVINGS  **VEGETARIAN**

NUTRITION TIP

Beans are more than just a meat substitute—they are considered both a vegetable and a protein. The latest dietary guidelines recommend we triple our current intake from 1 to 3 cups (250 to 625 mL) per week. Just 1 cup (250 mL) of beans supplies about 12 grams of fibre, which is half of your recommended daily intake.

FOR KIDS

Finely dice the mushrooms to make them more palatable for kids. Beans are a healthy source of protein for kids who don't eat meat or poultry.

NUTRITIONAL INFORMATION PER SERVING

Calories	123
Carbohydrates	13.4 g
Fibre	4.1 g
Protein	5.5 g
Fat	6.8 g
Saturated Fat	1.1 g
Cholesterol	24 mg
Sodium	236 mg

4 tsp (20 mL) vegetable oil, divided
12 oz (340 g) chopped button mushrooms
5 sliced green onions, divided
3 cloves garlic, divided
1 can (15 oz/444 mL) black beans, rinsed and drained
3 Tbsp (45 mL) fresh lemon juice
1 ½ Tbsp (22 mL) tahini paste
1 tsp (5 mL) Sriracha or your favourite hot sauce
½ tsp (2 mL) ground cumin
Salt and pepper

1 egg
3 Tbsp (45 mL) seasoned dry breadcrumbs
Fresh veggies, for garnish

AVOCADO CRÈME

½ avocado, halved, pitted, peeled and diced
1 Tbsp (15 mL) reduced-fat sour cream
1 Tbsp (15 mL) fresh lime juice
2 Tbsp (30 mL) fresh cilantro leaves
⅛ tsp (0.5 mL) salt
8 hamburger buns (optional)

1. Preheat the oven to 350°F (175°C). Line a baking sheet with foil and spray with vegetable oil.

2. In a large skillet over medium heat, heat 2 tsp (10 mL) of the oil. Add the mushrooms and cook, stirring occasionally, for 8 minutes, or just until browned. Transfer to a food processor.

3. Add 3 of the green onions, 2 of the garlic cloves, the beans, lemon juice, tahini, Sriracha, cumin, salt, pepper, egg and breadcrumbs. Pulse just until combined. Using your hands, form 8 patties.

4. In a large skillet over medium heat, heat the remaining 2 tsp (10 mL) of the oil. Working in batches, sear the patties for 3 minutes per side, until browned. Transfer to the prepared baking sheet and bake for 10 minutes or just until warmed through.

5. Meanwhile, in a food processor, combine the remaining 2 green onions, avocado, sour cream, lemon juice, cilantro, remaining garlic clove and salt and purée until smooth.

6. Split the buns (if using) in half. Top the bottom halves with a veggie patty. Place a dollop of the avocado mixture on each patty and sandwich with the top halves of the buns. Serve.

LENTIL STEW WITH PEAS

Indian cuisine has become a staple in many kitchens. It is flavourful, delivers a variety of health benefits (due to the inclusion of spices such as turmeric, ginger and garlic, it's considered an antioxidant and anti-inflammatory) and is relatively inexpensive to prepare. I don't like my food too spicy, so I hold back on the seasonings, but you can tailor the spices to suit your taste buds. I like to use brown lentils rather than green because they cook in half the time.

MAKES 6 SERVINGS **GLUTEN FREE**  **VEGETARIAN**

NUTRITION TIP

Lentils help to lower cholesterol, reduce the risk of heart disease and stabilize your blood sugar (due to their high fibre content). Just 1 cup (250 mL) contains over 16 grams of fibre, which is close to three-quarters of your daily needs.

FOR KIDS

This recipe is very mild tasting, which makes it suitable for kids. If desired, you can reduce the amount of ginger and curry powder.

NUTRITIONAL INFORMATION PER SERVING (1½ CUPS/375 ML)

Calories	216
Carbohydrates	35.7 g
Fibre	10.7 g
Protein	10.8 g
Fat	3.7 g
Saturated Fat	1.3 g
Cholesterol	0.2 mg
Sodium	213 mg

2 tsp (10 mL) vegetable oil
1 cup (250 mL) diced onion
2 tsp (10 mL) minced peeled fresh ginger
1 tsp (5 mL) minced garlic
1 tsp (5 mL) curry powder
1 cup (250 mL) cubed (½ inch/1 cm) peeled potatoes
½ cup (125 mL) diced carrots
1 cup (250 mL) brown lentils
8 oz (230 g) canned diced tomatoes, with juice
¾ cup (185 mL) canned light coconut milk
3 cups (750 mL) reduced-sodium vegetable or chicken stock
1 cup (250 mL) frozen peas
Salt and pepper
3 cups (750 mL) cooked brown or white rice (optional)
¼ cup (60 mL) plain 1% yogurt (optional), for garnish
3 Tbsp (45 mL) chopped fresh cilantro leaves, for garnish

1. In a large saucepan over medium heat, heat the oil. Add the onion, ginger, garlic and curry powder. Cook, stirring occasionally, for 5 minutes, until the onions are softened. Stir in the potatoes, carrots, lentils, tomatoes, coconut milk and stock. Cover, reduce the heat to low, and simmer for about 20 minutes or until the lentils are tender.

2. Add the peas, and salt and pepper, and stir to combine.

3. Serve over a bed of rice (if using) and garnish with yogurt (if using) and cilantro.

PASTA AND GRAINS

PASTAS AND GRAINS are consumed in every country in the world. We are spoilt for choice: rice, bulgur, quinoa, barley and a variety of grain pastas are readily available in most supermarkets. A few years ago the anti-carb movement lead us to believe that we should cut out these carbohydrates, but today we know better. Whole-wheat and ancient grains are an excellent source of fibre and protein. Fibre helps control blood sugar, lowers LDL (bad) cholesterol and reduces colon cancer risk.

For perfect pasta every time, cook it in a large pot of boiling water. Use 12 to 16 cups (3 to 4 L) of water per pound of pasta. Stir pasta occasionally while cooking and cook just until slightly firm to the bite (al dente). If serving hot drain and add sauce immediately. If serving cold drain and rinse with cold water. To reheat pasta run hot water over the pasta, drain well and immediately add to the sauce. For these recipes, approximately ½ lb (250 g) dry pasta serves 4 people, ¾ lb (375 g) serves 6 people, and 1 lb (500 g) serves 8 people.

Instructions for cooking grains vary by type of grain, so be sure to follow the instructions in the respective recipes.

For a great vegetarian one-pot dish, try Gnocchi with Squash, Kale and Parmesan (page 92). The kids will devour the Pizza Mac and Cheese Pie (page 97). Quinoa lovers should try "Fried" Quinoa with Shrimp (page 88).

QUINOA BITES

These mini quinoa patties make a great appetizer or a side dish. Instead of frying these in oil, I decided to bake them. The result was a crunchy exterior and moist interior. Tahini is sesame seed paste similar to nut butter; if you don't have any, you can substitute almond or peanut butter.

PREP TIME:
10
MINUTES

COOK TIME:
27
MINUTES

MAKES 14 BITES  **VEGETARIAN**

NUTRITION TIP

Quinoa is a super food: It's the only grain that is a complete protein. It's also naturally gluten-free. Interesting fact: NASA considers quinoa an ideal food for long-duration space flights!

FOR KIDS

Quinoa is hypoallergenic, making it a good choice for children with food sensitivities.

NUTRITIONAL INFORMATION PER SERVING (1 PIECE)

Calories	63
Carbohydrates	6.6 g
Fibre	0.7 g
Protein	2.7 g
Fat	3 g
Saturated Fat	0.8 g
Cholesterol	16 mg
Sodium	124 mg

1 ½ (375 mL) cups water or reduced-sodium vegetarian stock

½ cup (125 mL) quinoa, rinsed and drained

¼ cup (60 mL) shredded carrot

¼ cup (60 mL) sliced green onions

¼ cup (60 mL) chopped rehydrated sun-dried tomatoes (see Tip, page 19)

1 egg

1 ½ oz (45 g) crumbled light feta cheese

2 Tbsp (30 mL) all-purpose flour

1 Tbsp (15 mL) tahini

1 Tbsp (15 mL) fresh lemon juice

3 Tbsp (45 mL) chopped fresh cilantro or basil leaves

Salt and pepper

2 tsp (10 mL) vegetable oil

GARNISH

½ cup (125 mL) tzatziki (store-bought)

1. Preheat the oven to 425°F (220°C). Line a baking sheet with foil and lightly spray it with vegetable oil.

2. Bring the water or stock to a boil in a small saucepan. Add the quinoa, cover, reduce the heat to low and simmer for 15 minutes, until the quinoa is tender. Drain any excess liquid.

3. In a food processor, combine the carrot, onions, sun-dried tomatoes, egg, feta, flour, tahini, lemon juice, cilantro, salt, pepper and cooked quinoa. Process just until the mixture sticks together, scraping down the sides of the work bowl as necessary (do not purée).

4. Using your hands, form 14 small patties (about 2 Tbsp/30 mL each). Transfer the patties to the prepared baking sheet and lightly spray with vegetable oil. Bake for 12 minutes, turning over after 8 minutes, until lightly browned.

5. Serve with the tzatziki.

"FRIED" QUINOA WITH SHRIMP

Traditional Chinese fried rice is delicious, but has little nutrition and is packed with calories and fat. My version of "fried" quinoa is outstanding and super healthy. I've added finely diced eggplant, morsels of shrimp and edamame for a complete one-dish meal. You can use pre-cooked baby cocktail shrimp instead of cooking larger shrimp.

PREP TIME:
15
MINUTES

COOK TIME:
15
MINUTES

MAKES 6 SERVINGS **DAIRY FREE**

NUTRITION TIP

Green peas are traditionally added to fried rice, but edamame have four times the protein. One cup (250 mL) of peas contains 8 grams of protein; the same amount of edamame contains a whopping 33 grams!

FOR KIDS

Some children don't enjoy the texture of eggplant. If desired, you can substitute finely diced zucchini for the eggplant. You can also substitute diced chicken for the shrimp.

NUTRITIONAL INFORMATION PER SERVING

Calories	268
Carbohydrates	29 g
Fibre	4.7 g
Protein	21 g
Fat	7.2 g
Saturated Fat	0.8 g
Cholesterol	111 mg
Sodium	443 mg

1 cup (250 mL) quinoa, rinsed and drained
1 ½ cups (375 mL) water
2 tsp (10 mL) vegetable oil
1 cup (250 mL) diced onion
3 cups (750 mL) diced unpeeled eggplant
1 ½ tsp (7 mL) minced garlic
2 tsp (10 mL) minced peeled fresh ginger
12 oz (340 g) peeled and deveined shrimp, diced
1 cup (250 mL) shelled edamame
1 cup (250 mL) grated carrots
3 Tbsp (45 mL) reduced-sodium soy sauce
1 Tbsp (15 mL) sesame oil
⅓ cup (80 mL) sliced green onions

1. In a large saucepan, combine the quinoa and water and bring to a boil. Cover, reduce the heat to low and simmer for 15 minutes, until the quinoa is light and fluffy and the water has been absorbed.

2. Meanwhile, in a large skillet over medium-high heat, heat the oil. Add the onion and eggplant and sauté for about 10 minutes, just until the eggplant is tender. Stir in the garlic, ginger and shrimp and sauté for 3 minutes, just until the shrimp is opaque and cooked through.

3. Add the edamame, carrot, soy sauce, sesame oil, cooked quinoa and green onions. Stir to combine. Serve.

TEX-MEX BROWN RICE PATTIES

These rice patties are similar to a veggie burger, but use brown rice as the base. Sautéing the corn first lends a barbequed taste and texture that works well in these Southwestern-inspired patties. The combination of brown rice and beans makes this a great option for vegetarians.

PREP TIME:
15
MINUTES

COOK TIME:
30
MINUTES

MAKES 4 SERVINGS  **VEGETARIAN**

NUTRITION TIP

Compared with 1 cup (250 mL) of white rice, which contains 0.6 grams of fibre, 1 cup (250 mL) of brown rice contains a whopping 3.5 grams of fibre. Brown rice is also a lower glycemic food, which means it stabilizes your blood sugar better than white rice.

FOR KIDS

Children will enjoy the sweet corn in these patties. You can always substitute white rice if brown rice is not yet on their list of likes. You can also sub in ketchup if the salsa or tzatziki doesn't appeal to them.

NUTRITIONAL INFORMATION PER SERVING (2 PATTIES)

Calories	224
Carbohydrates	33 g
Fibre	3 g
Protein	10 g
Fat	6.1 g
Saturated Fat	1.8 g
Cholesterol	7.6 mg
Sodium	360 mg

½ cup (125 mL) brown rice
1 cup (250 mL) reduced-sodium stock or water
2 tsp (10 mL) vegetable oil
½ cup (125 mL) chopped onion
1 tsp (5 mL) minced garlic
½ cup (125 mL) corn niblets (canned or frozen; if canned, rinsed and drained)
½ cup (125 mL) canned black beans, rinsed and drained
⅓ cup (80 mL) sliced green onions
¼ cup (60 mL) unseasoned dry breadcrumbs
½ cup (125 mL) shredded light cheddar cheese
2 Tbsp (30 mL) chopped fresh cilantro or flat-leaf parsley leaves
Salt and pepper
⅓ cup (80 mL) salsa or tzatziki (optional)

1. In a saucepan, bring the rice and stock to a boil. Cover, reduce the heat and simmer for 15 to 20 minutes or just until the rice is tender and the liquid has evaporated.

2. Meanwhile, in a small skillet over medium-high heat, heat the oil. Add the onion, garlic and corn and cook, stirring occasionally, just until corn is lightly browned, about 5 minutes. Transfer the mixture to a food processor and add the beans, onions, breadcrumbs, cheese, cilantro, salt and pepper and cooked rice. Pulse the mixture just until it begins to hold together (do not purée).

3. Using your hands, form 8 patties.

4. Heat a large skillet over medium heat. Lightly spray it with vegetable oil and, working in batches if necessary (so as not to crowd the pan), cook each patty for about 3 minutes per side, just until browned and heated through.

5. Serve with either salsa or tzatziki (if using).

OVEN-BAKED RISOTTO WITH KALE PESTO

Risotto is a Northern Italian dish of rice cooked in broth to a creamy consistency. Traditionally you have to stir the rice constantly for about 15 minutes while cooking, but in my version you bake it in the oven, which gives you a rich and creamy consistency without all of the stirring. The kale pesto is what puts this risotto over the top.

PREP TIME:
15
MINUTES

COOK TIME:
13
MINUTES

MAKES 4 SERVINGS  VEGETARIAN

NUTRITION TIP

Arborio rice is a better source of fibre than long-grain rice. It contains 2 grams per serving compared with 0.6 grams in long-grain rice. Fibre in food helps with hunger control (it keeps you feeling full for longer), and getting more in your diet may lower your risk of heart disease, type 2 diabetes and obesity.

FOR KIDS

Kale contains calcium, which is great for a child's bones and teeth. If your child hasn't been won over by kale just yet, substitute baby kale or spinach, which have a much milder taste than regular varieties of kale.

NUTRITIONAL INFORMATION PER SERVING

Calories	438
Carbohydrates	50 g
Fibre	4.2 g
Protein	11.4 g
Fat	20.3 g
Saturated Fat	3.2 g
Cholesterol	6.6 mg
Sodium	256 mg

2 tsp (10 mL) vegetable oil

1 ½ cup (375 mL) diced onion

2 tsp (10 mL) minced garlic

1 cup (250 mL) Arborio or other short-grain rice

½ cup (125 mL) dry white wine

2 ¾ cups (685 mL) hot reduced-sodium vegetable or chicken stock, divided

PESTO

1 cup (250 mL) lightly packed fresh flat-leaf parsley leaves

1 cup (250 mL) loosely packed baby kale leaves

3 Tbsp (45 mL) extra virgin olive oil

3 Tbsp (45 mL) toasted pine nuts or almonds (see Tip, page 35)

6 Tbsp (90 mL) freshly grated Parmesan cheese, divided

2 Tbsp (30 mL) water

Salt and pepper

1. Preheat the oven to 350°F (175°C).

2. In a large ovenproof skillet over medium-high heat, heat the vegetable oil. Add the onion and garlic and cook for about 5 minutes, until softened. Add the rice and cook, stirring, for 1 minute. Add the wine and bring to a boil, stirring up any browned bits from the bottom of the pan. Add 2 cups (500 mL) of the hot stock, bring to a simmer, then cover and bake in the preheated oven for 15 minutes, until the rice is tender.

3. Meanwhile, in a food processor, combine the parsley, kale, olive oil, nuts, 3 Tbsp (45 mL) of the Parmesan, water, and salt and pepper until smooth, scraping down the sides of the work bowl as needed.

4. Place the skillet over medium heat. Stir in the remaining ¾ cup (185 mL) stock and kale pesto, and cook until heated through. Serve, garnished with the remaining cheese.

MEDITERRANEAN COUSCOUS

Israeli couscous—also called pearl pasta—is a type of pasta made from semolina or wheat flour that is shaped into small balls. It has a nutty flavour and chewy texture. It's so versatile that you can use it in any recipe that calls for pasta, rice or other grains. I love it in this Mediterranean-influenced dish. Serve it on its own or try adding some grilled protein such as chicken or fish. Serve warm or cold.

PREP TIME:
15
MINUTES

COOK TIME:
8
MINUTES

MAKES 6 SERVINGS  VEGETARIAN

NUTRITION TIP

Using whole-wheat Israeli couscous will increase the protein and fibre content.

FOR KIDS

Kids love the texture of this variety of couscous, which is larger than regular couscous. If desired, omit the olives and red onions (try green onions). If the kids don't like feta, use shredded light mozzarella cheese.

NUTRITIONAL INFORMATION PER SERVING

Calories	181
Carbohydrates	22.8 g
Fibre	2.2 g
Protein	6.1 g
Fat	7.4 g
Saturated Fat	1.9 g
Cholestero	4.2 mg
Sodium	240 mg

1 cup (250 mL) Israeli couscous (pearl pasta)

1 cup (250 mL) diced green bell pepper

1 cup (250 mL) diced seeded tomatoes

⅓ cup (80 mL) diced red onion

¼ cup (60 mL) chopped pitted black olives

3 oz (90 g) crumbled light feta cheese

2 Tbsp (30 mL) extra virgin olive oil

2 Tbsp (30 mL) fresh lemon juice

1 tsp (5 mL) minced garlic

Freshly ground black pepper

¼ cup (60 mL) chopped fresh basil or mint leaves

1. In a pot of boiling water, cook couscous for about 8 minutes, just until tender. Drain and rinse under cold running water, if serving cold. Drain well and transfer to a serving bowl.

2. Add the green pepper, tomato, onion, olives, cheese, oil, juice, garlic, pepper and basil. Toss well. Serve.

GNOCCHI WITH SQUASH, KALE AND PARMESAN

Gnocchi, which means "dumpling" in Italian, is a made from a soft potato dough. It's true comfort food. Although it's tasty in a simple tomato sauce, here I've paired it with cubes of butternut squash, kale and two cheeses to make it a heartier—and more nutritious—dish. The vegetables and cheese keep the gnocchi moist, so no sauce is needed. If you like a more flavourful cheese than Parmesan, try Romano, Asiago or Pecorino.

PREP TIME:
10
MINUTES

COOK TIME:
18
MINUTES

MAKES 6 SERVINGS  **VEGETARIAN**

NUTRITION TIP

Butternut squash is filled with vitamins A and C, potassium and fibre. Kale is a cancer-fighting cruciferous vegetable that contains our daily amounts of vitamins K, C and A.

FOR KIDS

Try making this with either baby kale or spinach, which tend to be sweeter and slightly more tender than large kale leaves.

NUTRITIONAL INFORMATION PER SERVING

Calories	234
Carbohydrates	41 g
Fibre	4.1 g
Protein	10.2 g
Fat	4.5 g
Saturated Fat	2.1 g
Cholesterol	12 mg
Sodium	625 mg

1 tsp (5 mL) vegetable oil
1 cup (250 mL) diced onion
1½ tsp (7 mL) minced garlic
Salt and pepper
1½ cup (375 mL) diced peeled butternut squash
1 cup (250 mL) diced red bell pepper

1 lb (500 g) gnocchi (about 1¾ cups/435 mL; see Tip)
8 cups (2 L) lightly packed chopped trimmed kale leaves
¾ cup (185 mL) freshly grated Parmesan cheese
⅓ cup (80 mL) shredded light mozzarella cheese

1. Preheat the oven to 425°F (220°C). Spray a 9- × 13-inch (23 × 33 cm) casserole dish with vegetable oil.

2. In a large skillet over medium heat, heat the oil. Add the onion and cook for about 3 minutes, until softened. Add the garlic, salt, pepper, squash and red pepper and cook for 5 minutes, stirring often, until the squash is tender. Transfer to a large bowl.

3. Meanwhile, bring a pot of water to a boil. Add the gnocchi and return the water to a boil. Boil for 4 or 5 minutes, just until the gnocchi rise to the surface and are tender. Stir in the kale during last 2 minutes of cooking. Drain well.

4. Add the cooked gnocchi and kale to the squash mixture and gently toss to combine. Sprinkle with the Parmesan, and gently toss to combine.

5. Transfer the gnocchi mixture to the prepared baking dish. Top with the mozzarella. Bake for 5 minutes or just until the cheese has melted.

TIP You can find premade gnocchi in the refrigerated section of well-stocked supermarkets.

GNOCCHI WITH PARSLEY FETA PESTO

Gnocchi has a plump, pillowy texture and mild, delicate flavour that pairs well with pesto. When basil is out of season or too expensive, parsley is a wonderful substitute. Feta adds a pleasing tang. For a stronger herb flavour, you can use a combination of half each basil and parsley.

PREP TIME:
5
MINUTES

COOK TIME:
5
MINUTES

MAKES 4 SERVINGS  **VEGETARIAN**

NUTRITION TIP

Traditional pesto is high in calories and fat due to the amount of olive oil used. Just ¼ cup (60 mL) of store-bought pesto has 240 calories and 24 grams of fat compared with my parsley version, which contains 150 calories and 11 grams of fat.

FOR KIDS

Most children love this dish, but if you have a very picky eater, you may want to substitute Parmesan or a milder semi-hard cheese such as brick or cheddar for the feta.

NUTRITIONAL INFORMATION PER SERVING

Calories	287
Carbohydrates	31 g
Fibre	1.6 g
Protein	7.6 g
Fat	15.5 g
Saturated Fat	2.7 g
Cholesterol	3.3 mg
Sodium	554 mg

12 oz (340 g) potato gnocchi (about 1 ¾ cups/435 mL)

PARSLEY FETA PESTO

¾ cup (185 mL) chopped fresh flat-leaf parsley leaves

2 oz (60 g) crumbled light feta cheese

1 small clove garlic

Pinch coarse black pepper

3 Tbsp (45 mL) extra virgin olive oil

2 Tbsp (30 mL) water

GARNISH

¼ cup (60 mL) toasted sliced blanched almonds (see Tip, page 35)

1. Bring a large pot of water to a boil. Add the gnocchi and return the water to a boil. Boil for 4 or 5 minutes, just until the gnocchi rise to the surface and are tender. Drain well and transfer to a serving bowl.

2. Meanwhile, in a food processor, combine the parsley, feta, garlic, pepper, oil and water and process until smooth, scraping down the sides of the work bowl as necessary. If pesto seems too thick, add water, a tablespoon (15 mL) at a time, until the desired consistency is reached.

3. Pour the pesto over the cooked gnocchi and toss to coat well. Garnish with toasted almonds. Serve.

CHICKEN AND EGGPLANT PASTA PARMESAN

Eggplant parmesan and chicken parmesan are traditional Italian dishes. I decided to combine them with pasta to make this delicious and easy-to-prepare one-bowl meal. Keep the eggplant and chicken pieces small—they will cook faster. Reserve some of the pasta cooking water to add to the pan before finishing—this will add flavour without fat.

PREP TIME:
15 MINUTES

COOK TIME:
15 MINUTES

MAKES 6 SERVINGS **DAIRY FREE**  **GLUTEN FREE**  **VEGETARIAN**

NUTRITION TIP

Many of the nutritional benefits in eggplant come from the skin, which is full of fibre, potassium, magnesium and antioxidants, so don't peel it!

FOR KIDS

If your children don't like eggplant, try making this with zucchini, which has a milder flavour. You may also want to finely dice the vegetables, which may make it more enjoyable for kids to eat.

NUTRITIONAL INFORMATION PER SERVING

Calories	455
Carbohydrates	55 g
Fibre	9.1 g
Protein	27 g
Fat	14.8 g
Saturated Fat	4.3 g
Cholesterol	96 mg
Sodium	795 mg

2 eggs

2 Tbsp (30 mL) 2% milk

⅔ cup (160 mL) unseasoned dry breadcrumbs

3 cups (750 mL) diced (½ inch/1 cm) eggplant (unpeeled)

8 oz (230 g) skinless, boneless chicken breast, diced

2 ¾ cups (685 mL) tomato sauce (store-bought or homemade)

1 ¼ cups (310 mL) reduced-sodium chicken stock

8 oz (230 g) whole-grain rotini or penne pasta

1 cup (250 mL) shredded light mozzarella cheese

¼ cup (60 mL) freshly grated Parmesan cheese

¼ cup (60 mL) chopped fresh basil leaves

1. Preheat the oven to 425°F (220°C). Line a large baking sheet with foil and lightly spray it with vegetable oil.

2. In a shallow bowl, combine the eggs and milk. In another shallow bowl, place the breadcrumbs.

3. Working in batches, dip the eggplant in the milk mixture, turning to coat well, then in the crumb mixture, coating both sides. Place on the prepared baking sheet. Repeat with the chicken.

4. Bake for 15 to 20 minutes or just until the chicken is cooked through and the eggplant is tender and lightly browned.

5. Meanwhile, in a saucepan, combine the pasta sauce and stock and heat until warmed through.

6. In a pot of boiling water, cook the pasta according to the package instructions, just until slightly firm to the bite (al dente). Drain well and transfer to a serving bowl.

7. Add the baked eggplant and chicken, warm pasta sauce mixture, both cheeses and basil. Toss to combine. Serve.

PIZZA MAC AND CHEESE PIE

Two of our favourite fast foods are pizza and mac and cheese. So why not combine these two things, but in a healthier way? A little experimentation in the kitchen and Pizza Mac and Cheese Pie was born! Instead of a doughy pizza crust base, I use whole-wheat penne pasta and pour a light cheese sauce over top. The cheese sauce is made with evaporated milk and chicken stock thickened with flour, which eliminates the use of excess butter and higher-fat milk. Using a sharp cheese amps up the flavour and allows you to use less, which also lowers the overall calories and fat.

PREP TIME:
10
MINUTES

COOK TIME:
30
MINUTES

MAKES 6 SERVINGS

NUTRITION TIP

Using a lower-fat cheese makes a big difference in overall calories and fat. Just 1 cup (250 mL) of regular cheddar cheese contains 455 calories and 37 grams of fat compared with the same amount of light cheddar, which contains only 195 calories and 8 grams of fat.

FOR KIDS

Just one serving of this dish delivers 19 grams of protein to your child!

NUTRITIONAL INFORMATION PER SERVING

Calories	357
Carbohydrates	53 g
Fibre	5.7 g
Protein	19.2 g
Fat	8.2 g
Saturated Fat	5 g
Cholesterol	23 mg
Sodium	399 mg

12 oz (340 g) penne pasta (preferably whole-wheat)

CHEESE SAUCE

2 Tbsp (30 mL) all-purpose flour

¾ cup (185 mL) reduced-sodium chicken or vegetable stock

¾ cup (185 mL) canned 2% evaporated milk

1 cup (250 mL) shredded light sharp (old) cheddar cheese

¼ cup (60 mL) freshly grated Parmesan cheese

½ tsp (2 mL) Dijon mustard

TOPPING

½ cup (125 mL) tomato sauce (store-bought or homemade)

½ cup (125 mL) sliced green bell peppers

½ cup (125 mL) cherry tomatoes, halved

½ cup (125 mL) shredded light mozzarella cheese

1. Preheat the oven to 375°F (190°C). Lightly spray a 10-inch (25 cm) ovenproof skillet or pie pan with vegetable oil.

2. In a large pot of boiling water, cook the penne according to the package instructions, just until slightly firm to the bite (al dente). Drain the pasta well and transfer to the prepared pie dish.

3. **Make sauce:** Meanwhile, in a saucepan over medium heat, whisk together the flour, stock and milk until smooth. Cook, whisking constantly, for about 3 minutes or until the mixture is slightly thickened and heated through.

4. Stir in the cheddar and Parmesan, and the mustard. Cook until the cheese melts, about 1 minute. Remove from the heat. Pour the cheese sauce over the pasta and toss to combine.

5. Using a rubber spatula, flatten the pasta in the pan. Top with the tomato sauce, green peppers, tomatoes and mozzarella cheese. Bake in the preheated oven for 25 minutes, until heated through and cheese is melted and bubbling. Remove from the oven and let rest for at least 5 minutes before cutting into individual portions.

MEXICAN CHICKEN LASAGNA

Lasagna is a family favourite, but I decided to give it a Tex-Mex twist by substituting the small soft corn tortillas I found in in supermarket for the lasagne noodles. The result is exceptional. If you can't find corn tortillas, use the flour ones.

PREP TIME:
15
MINUTES

COOK TIME:
28
MINUTES

MAKES 8 SERVINGS

NUTRITION TIP

Corn tortillas are healthier than flour tortillas. They are lower in fat and contain double the fibre and three times the magnesium.

FOR KIDS

Poultry contains an essential amino acid called tryptophan, which helps children relax and stay calm.

NUTRITIONAL INFORMATION PER SERVING	
Calories	384
Carbohydrates	24 g
Fibre	4 g
Protein	28 mg
Fat	21 g
Saturated Fat	6 g
Cholesterol	98 mg
Sodium	680 mg

2 tsp (10 mL) vegetable oil
1 cup (250 mL) diced onion
¾ cup (185 mL) diced red bell pepper
1 tsp (5 mL) minced garlic
1 small jalapeño pepper, seeded and minced
2 tsp (10 mL) chili powder
½ tsp (2 mL) ground cumin
1 lb (500 g) ground chicken
¾ cup (185 mL) canned black beans, rinsed and drained
1 cup (250 mL) tomato sauce (store-bought or homemade)
½ cup (125 mL) reduced-sodium chicken stock
½ cup (125 mL) medium salsa

1 ½ cups (375 mL) light ricotta cheese
2 cups (500 mL) shredded light sharp (old) cheddar cheese, divided
⅓ cup (80 mL) freshly grated Parmesan cheese
1 egg
¼ cup (60 mL) 2% milk
Salt and pepper
6 small (6 inches/15 cm) corn or flour tortillas

GARNISH (OPTIONAL)

½ cup (125 mL) diced seeded tomatoes
1 cup (250 mL) shredded romaine lettuce

1. Preheat the oven to 375°F (190°C). Lightly spray a 9- × 13-inch (23 × 33 cm) baking dish with vegetable oil.

2. In a large skillet over medium-high heat, heat the oil. Add the onion, bell pepper, garlic, jalapeño, chili and cumin and cook, stirring occasionally, for about 8 minutes. Add the chicken and cook, stirring occasionally for about 5 minutes.

3. Stir in the beans, tomato sauce, stock and salsa. Cover, reduce the heat and simmer for about 5 minutes, until slightly thickened.

4. In a bowl, combine the ricotta, 1 cup (250 mL) of cheddar, Parmesan, egg, milk, and salt and pepper.

5. Cut each tortilla into 4 wedges. Arrange 8 wedges evenly over the bottom of dish. Spread half the chicken mixture over top, followed by half of the cheese mixture. Cover with another 8 tortilla wedges. Repeat layers of the remaining chicken and cheese mixtures. End with a final layer of the remaining tortilla wedges. Sprinkle with the remaining 1 cup (250 mL) cheddar cheese. Bake for 20 minutes. Sprinkle with garnishes.

SOBA NOODLES WITH CHICKEN AND EDAMAME

Soba noodles are a healthy and delicious alternative to regular white noodles. They are made from buckwheat flour and have a nutty flavour that works well with the Asian flavours they are often served with. Here I pair them with edamame and chicken with a flavourful orange cilantro dressing for a tasty and easy cold or warm meal. I dust the chicken with flour before cooking, which keeps the meat super moist.

PREP TIME:
15
MINUTES

COOK TIME:
5
MINUTES

MAKES 4 SERVINGS **DAIRY FREE**

NUTRITION TIP

Soba noodles contain about 110 calories per 1 cup (250 mL), which is about half what regular wheat pasta contains. They are also rich in manganese, which helps strengthen our bones and is a powerful antioxidant.

FOR KIDS

Soba noodles are a good source of fibre for children. You can omit the hot sauce and increase the quantity of honey by 1 tsp (5 mL) for a little extra sweetness, if desired.

NUTRITIONAL INFORMATION PER SERVING

Calories	394
Carbohydrates	57.1 g
Fibre	1.7 g
Protein	23.2 g
Fat	9.0 g
Saturated Fat	1.1 g
Cholesterol	23.5 mg
Sodium	470.9 mg

6 oz (175 g) boneless, skinless chicken breast, cut into ¼-inch (6 mm) cubes
2 Tbsp (30 mL) all-purpose flour
2 tsp (10 mL) vegetable oil
6 oz (175 g) dried soba noodles or whole-wheat spaghetti pasta
1 cup (250 mL) shelled edamame beans
1 cup (250 mL) grated carrot

DRESSING

3 Tbsp (45 mL) orange juice
3 Tbsp (45 mL) chopped green onions
¼ cup (60 mL) chopped fresh cilantro or basil leaves
2 Tbsp (30 mL) reduced-sodium soy sauce
2 Tbsp (30 mL) liquid honey
1 Tbsp (15 mL) sesame oil
1 Tbsp (15 mL) mirin or sweet rice wine vinegar
2 tsp (10 mL) minced garlic
1 Tbsp (15 mL) minced peeled fresh ginger
2 tsp (10 mL) Sriracha or your favourite hot sauce
2 tsp (10 mL) toasted sesame seeds (see Tip, page 35)

1. Place the chicken and flour in a resealable bag or a bowl and toss to coat well.

2. In a small skillet over medium-high heat, heat the vegetable oil. Add the coated chicken and cook, stirring occasionally, for 5 minutes or just until lightly browned and cooked through.

3. Meanwhile, in a pot of boiling water, cook the soba noodles just until tender, 3 to 4 minutes. During the last minute of cooking, stir in the edamame. Drain and rinse well under cold running water, if serving cold. Transfer to a bowl along with the cooked chicken and carrot.

4. **Make the dressing:** In a bowl, combine the orange juice, onions, cilantro or basil, soy sauce, honey, sesame oil, mirin, garlic, ginger and hot sauce.

5. Pour the dressing over the noodles, toss until well coated, and garnish with sesame seeds. Serve.

FISH AND SEAFOOD

LONG GONE ARE the days when frozen sole or cod fillets, fish sticks and cocktail shrimp were the only choice. In most urban centres today a variety of fresh fish and seafood is readily available in grocery stores and fish markets. Fresh is always better than frozen.

Over the past 20 years fish and seafood consumption has increased by one-third. A focus on healthy eating, improvements in refrigeration and transportation (many fish are flash-frozen at sea), home grilling trends and the seduction of sushi have all contributed to its rise in popularity. And a good thing too: Fish and seafood are some of the healthiest proteins for your heart and brain. But sustainability is an important issue. Question your fishmonger about whether the fish comes from a sustainable source. Consult the Ocean Wise website, which can help you make informed decisions about your fish and seafood purchases.

Fresh fish has a bright colour, does not smell "fishy" and is not slimy. As soon as you get fish home, rinse it under cold running water, pat dry, wrap in plastic wrap and refrigerate for up to 2 days. If you have to freeze your fish, wrap it tightly in plastic wrap before freezing; darker oilier fish will keep for up to 4 months and lean fish up to 2 months in the freezer.

Try Hoisin Salmon with Ginger Slaw (page 114), a delicious salmon burger with a quick and easy slaw seasoned with soy sauce, sesame oil and ginger. If you like sushi, you'll love my variation on it: Sesame Tuna with Edamame and Soba Noodles (page 107) is a popular entrée.

THAI COCONUT CURRY SHRIMP

Curries are a perennial favourite. There are a number of good-quality premade curry pastes available (I prefer Thai Kitchen brand). Green curry paste is much hotter than red, so use whichever suits your tastes. If using frozen shrimp, be sure to defrost and drain well before weighing for this recipe.

PREP TIME:
10 MINUTES

COOK TIME:
11 MINUTES

MAKES 4 SERVINGS **DAIRY FREE**

NUTRITION TIP

Chili peppers are rich in vitamins A and C, making them a potent antioxidant and immune system-builder. They also stimulate digestion and circulation.

FOR KIDS

You can add 1 to 2 tsp (5 to 10 mL) of liquid honey to the sauce to slightly sweeten. Use red curry paste, which is much milder, and soy sauce instead of fish sauce.

NUTRITIONAL INFORMATION PER SERVING

Calories	352
Carbohydrates	19.1 g
Fibre	3.1 g
Protein	43.6 g
Fat	11.7 g
Saturated Fat	4.5 g
Cholesterol	321 mg
Sodium	658 mg

1 ½ lb (750 g) large shrimp, shelled (leave tail on) and deveined
2 tsp (10 mL) vegetable oil
2 cups (500 mL) sliced onions
2 Tbsp (30 mL) green or red curry paste, or to taste
1 Tbsp (15 mL) minced peeled fresh ginger
1 ½ tsp (7 mL) minced garlic
2 cups (500 mL) sliced red bell peppers
1 ½ cups (375 mL) canned light coconut milk
2 Tbsp (30 mL) all-purpose flour
1 Tbsp (15 mL) fish sauce or reduced-sodium soy sauce
1 tsp (5 mL) brown sugar
3 cups (750 mL) cooked rice or 4 oz (120 g) cooked rice noodles (optional)

GARNISH
¼ cup (60 mL) chopped unsalted roasted cashews
3 Tbsp (45 mL) chopped fresh cilantro leaves

1. Heat a large skillet over medium-high heat. Lightly spray the hot skillet with vegetable oil, and sauté the shrimp for 3 minutes or just until opaque and no longer pink. Transfer the shrimp to a plate.

2. In the same skillet, heat the oil. Add the onions, curry paste, ginger and garlic and sauté for 3 minutes, until fragrant. Add the red pepper and sauté for 2 minutes, until softened.

3. Meanwhile, in a bowl, whisk together the coconut milk, flour, fish sauce and sugar and until smooth. Stir into the onion mixture along with the cooked shrimp and cook just until sauce has thickened slightly, about 3 minutes.

4. Serve over cooked rice or noodles (if using) and garnish with chopped cashews and cilantro.

ORANGE SESAME SCALLOPS WITH RICE NOODLES

Scallops are the sweetest-tasting seafood from the ocean and are considered a delicacy. I prefer large sea scallops rather than small bay scallops, which can easily be overcooked and dried out. If using thawed frozen scallops, pat dry with a paper towel before cooking—they will sear better if dry.

PREP TIME:
10
MINUTES

COOK TIME:
6
MINUTES

MAKES 4 SERVINGS **DAIRY FREE**

NUTRITION TIP

Scallops are rich in omega-3 fatty acids, low in calories and a healthy source of protein. A 4-ounce (120 g) serving contains over a day's worth of vitamin B12, which is important for heart health.

FOR KIDS

If your kids don't like scallops, try making this dish with large shrimp instead. You can also serve this over rice or whole-grain spaghetti.

NUTRITIONAL INFORMATION PER SERVING

Calories	252
Carbohydrates	33.8 g
Fibre	0.2 g
Protein	19.7 g
Fat	3.3 g
Saturated Fat	0.4 g
Cholesterol	37.4 mg
Sodium	473 mg

4 oz (120 g) rice or soba noodles
⅓ cup (80 mL) chopped green onions
2 Tbsp (30 mL) reduced-sodium soy sauce
2 tsp (10 mL) sesame oil
1 ½ Tbsp (22 mL) orange juice
1 Tbsp (15 mL) liquid honey
1 ½ tsp (7 mL) rice wine vinegar
2 tsp (10 mL) minced peeled fresh ginger
1 tsp (5 mL) minced garlic
½ tsp (2 mL) Sriracha or your favourite hot sauce
1 lb (500 g) large scallops
2 Tbsp (30 mL) chopped fresh cilantro leaves, for garnish

1. In a large pot of boiling water, cook the noodles according to the package instructions, just until tender, about 4 minutes. Drain well and transfer to a large serving bowl. Add the green onions and toss to combine. Set aside.

2. Meanwhile, in a small bowl, whisk together the soy sauce, sesame oil, orange juice, honey, vinegar, ginger, garlic and Sriracha. Set aside.

3. Heat a skillet over medium-high heat. Lightly spray the skillet with vegetable oil. Add scallops and cook for about 1 minute per side, until browned. Add prepared sauce, bring to a boil and cook for another 2 to 3 minutes, just until scallops are cooked through (opaque).

4. Pour scallops and sauce over noodles. Garnish with cilantro. Serve.

ROLLED SOLE WITH PESTO AND FETA

Sole is a very mild fish and needs a boost of flavour to liven it up. I decided to roll the fillets with a pesto and cheese filling, and bake them in a light breading. You'll love the subtle flavours and tender texture. Serve with Date and Orange Arugula Salad with Pomegranate Dressing (see page 39).

PREP TIME:
10
MINUTES

COOK TIME:
10
MINUTES

MAKES 4 SERVINGS

NUTRITION TIP

Sole is one of the lowest-calorie and -fat fish. A 3 1/2-ounce (105 g) portion contains only 115 calories and 1 gram of fat, and is a great source of lean protein (only 24 grams).

FOR KIDS

Kids love mild fish, and sole is the perfect variety. Try a milder cheese such as shredded Havarti or firm brie.

NUTRITIONAL INFORMATION PER SERVING

Calories	220
Carbohydrates	11 g
Fibre	1 g
Protein	19.2 g
Fat	10.6 g
Saturated Fat	3.3 g
Cholesterol	99 mg
Sodium	580 mg

½ cup (125 mL) unseasoned dry breadcrumbs

2 Tbsp (30 mL) freshly grated Parmesan cheese

1 egg

2 Tbsp (30 mL) 2% milk

⅓ cup (80 mL) pesto sauce (see recipe page 33 or store-bought)

1½ oz (45 g) crumbled light feta cheese

4 sole fillets (skinless; about 4 oz/120 g each)

1. Preheat the oven to 425°F (220°C). Line a baking sheet with foil and lightly spray with vegetable oil.

2. Prepare a breading station: Combine breadcrumbs and Parmesan in a shallow bowl. In another shallow bowl, whisk together the egg and milk.

3. In a bowl, combine pesto and feta. Spread evenly on top of fillets. Starting from the narrow end, roll each fillet into a cylinder.

4. Dip each roll into the egg mixture then roll the crumbs until well coated. Place seam-side down on the prepared baking sheet. Bake in the preheated oven for 10 to 12 minutes or just until the fish reaches an internal temperature of 130°F (54°C).

SESAME TUNA WITH EDAMAME AND SOBA NOODLES

Searing fresh tuna is the most delectable way to prepare this nutritious fish. Because the tuna is served rare, be sure to purchase fresh sushi-quality tuna or Ahi tuna. The key to maintaining tenderness is to quickly sear the outside of the fish, just to warm it, and to slice it against the grain. If you are not serving the fish immediately, place it in the refrigerator to cool down and stop the cooking process. Before serving, remove from the fridge and bring to room temperature.

PREP TIME:
5
MINUTES

COOK TIME:
5
MINUTES

MAKES 4 SERVINGS **DAIRY FREE**

NUTRITION TIP

Buckwheat noodles, also known as soba noodles, are a good source of manganese, lean protein and complex carbohydrates. They are also gluten-free.

FOR KIDS

Most children do not enjoy seared tuna, so try serving the soba noodles with salmon or a mild white fish such as tilapia instead. You can also substitute the soba noodles with whole-wheat spaghettini and substitute green peas for the edamame.

NUTRITIONAL INFORMATION PER SERVING

Calories	368
Carbohydrates	30.1 g
Fibre	0.9 g
Protein	36.7 g
Fat	11.1 g
Saturated Fat	2.0 g
Cholesterol	41.7 mg
Sodium	468 mg

4 oz (120 g) dried soba noodles
1 cup (250 mL) frozen shelled edamame
1 Tbsp (15 mL) toasted sesame seeds (see Tip, page 35)
1 tuna steak (12 oz/340 g)
2 Tbsp (30 mL) reduced-sodium soy sauce
1 Tbsp (15 mL) fresh lemon juice
1 Tbsp (15 mL) sweet chili sauce or ketchup
1 Tbsp (15 mL) sesame oil
1 tsp (5 mL) liquid honey
¼ cup (60 mL) chopped fresh cilantro leaves

1. In a large pot of boiling water, cook the noodles according to the package instructions, just until tender (about 3 minutes). Add the edamame to the pot during the last minute of cooking (they should turn bright green when cooked). Drain well and transfer to a serving platter.

2. Meanwhile, place the sesame seeds in a shallow dish. Press each side of the tuna in the sesame seeds to coat well.

3. Preheat a grill pan over high heat. Place the coated tuna on the grill and sear, without moving, to form a light crust (tuna should still be pink or rare on the inside), 1 to 2 minutes. Flip over and sear the other side for 1 to 2 minutes. Remove from heat and slice thinly across the grain.

4. In a bowl, whisk together the soy sauce, lemon juice, sweet chili sauce, sesame oil, honey and cilantro. Pour all but 1 Tbsp (15 mL) over the noodles and toss until noodles are well coated. Top with sliced tuna. Drizzle with the reserved sauce. Serve.

PHYLLO TROUT WITH GOAT CHEESE AND OLIVES

Rather than wrapping a piece of fish in phyllo, I decided to simply cut some phyllo into strands and bake it on top of the fish. The result is not only delicious, but beautiful. There really isn't an easier way to jazz up a fish fillet. (You can wrap the unused phyllo in plastic wrap and refreeze.) Serve with steamed broccoli.

PREP TIME:
5
MINUTES

COOK TIME:
12
MINUTES

MAKES 4 SERVINGS

NUTRITION TIP

Phyllo is a low-fat and low-calorie pastry dough, but when it is brushed with butter or oil the calories and fat increase exponentially! The key is to lightly spray every other phyllo sheet with vegetable oil, which will only add minimal amount of calories and fat.

FOR KIDS

Kids love the soft texture and milky flavour of trout. Use a mild cheese such as shredded Havarti or mozzarella. Omit the olives.

NUTRITIONAL INFORMATION PER SERVING

Calories	380
Carbohydrates	11 g
Fibre	0.4 g
Protein	35 g
Fat	18 g
Saturated Fat	5.0 g
Cholesterol	75 mg
Sodium	341 mg

4 trout fillets (skin-on; 6 oz/175 g each)
2 oz (60 g) crumbled light goat or feta cheese
¼ cup (60 mL) chopped pitted black or green olives
2 sheets phyllo pastry

1. Preheat the oven to 400°F (200°C). Line a baking sheet with foil and lightly spray with vegetable oil. Arrange the fish on the prepared baking sheet.

2. In a small bowl, combine the goat cheese and olives. Spread evenly on top of each fillet.

3. Place the phyllo sheets on top of each other and, using a sharp knife, cut into 4 squares. Stack the squares on top of each other and roll tightly into a cylinder. Cut crosswise into thin strips.

4. Firmly press an even amount of phyllo strips on top of each piece of trout. Lightly spray with vegetable oil. Bake in the preheated oven for 12 minutes per inch of thickness, including the topping, or until the fish flakes easily with a fork (see page 112). Serve.

ALMOND BUTTER AND PANKO-CRUSTED TROUT

Recipes for peanut butter sauces and glazes abound, but almond butter is a delicious alternative, resulting in a milder and smoother-tasting sauce. Be sure to choose almond-only butter, since some nut butters can have added sugar. If you want to serve extra sauce with the fish, double the quantities for the sauce. Serve with sautéed sugar snap peas.

PREP TIME:
10
MINUTES

COOK TIME:
12
MINUTES

MAKES 4 SERVINGS **DAIRY FREE**

NUTRITION TIP

Almond butter is more nutritious than peanut butter. It contains four times more vitamin E, which neutralizes free radicals, and double the magnesium, which contributes to the functioning of your nervous system.

FOR KIDS

If your child doesn't have a tree nut allergy, almonds are perfect. For children with tree nut allergies, substitute an equal amount of soy butter.

NUTRITIONAL INFORMATION PER SERVING

Calories	288
Carbohydrates	10.5 g
Fibre	1.4 g
Protein	30.5 g
Fat	12.9 g
Saturated Fat	0.9 g
Cholesterol	82 mg
Sodium	466 mg

1 ½ Tbsp (22 mL) almond butter
1 Tbsp (15 mL) reduced-sodium soy sauce
1 Tbsp (15 mL) mirin or sweet rice wine vinegar
1 tsp (5 mL) liquid honey
½ tsp (2 mL) minced peeled fresh ginger
½ tsp (2 mL) minced garlic
½ tsp (2 mL) Sriracha or your favourite hot sauce

1 ½ lb (750 g) trout (skinless)
⅓ cup (80 mL) unseasoned panko or dry breadcrumbs
2 Tbsp (30 mL) chopped or sliced blanched almonds
1 tsp (5 mL) toasted sesame seeds (see Tip, page 35)
2 tsp (10 mL) sesame oil
Salt

1. Preheat the oven to 425°F (220°C). Line a baking sheet with foil and lightly spray with vegetable oil.

2. In a small bowl, whisk together the almond butter, soy sauce, mirin, honey, ginger, garlic and hot sauce until smooth.

3. Place fish on the prepared baking sheet and spread sauce evenly over top.

4. In a small bowl, combine the panko, almonds, sesame seeds, oil and salt. Sprinkle evenly over the fish and bake in the preheated oven for 12 minutes, until fish flakes easily with a fork and reaches an internal temperature of 130°F (54°C). Serve.

MUSHROOM- AND ALMOND-CRUSTED TILAPIA

A toasted mushroom topping is a delicious and creative way to serve this mild white fish. Use any variety of mushroom, such as button, oyster or cremini. When cooking mushrooms, sauté them over medium heat until the moisture has evaporated and the mushrooms are tender, otherwise they will steam, leaving them too wet. Serve with grilled asparagus.

PREP TIME:
10
MINUTES

COOK TIME:
15
MINUTES

MAKES 4 SERVINGS DAIRY FREE GLUTEN FREE

NUTRITION TIP

Tilapia is one of the leanest fish. It is low in calories and fat. Look for farmed tilapia from the United States, which is a sustainable option.

FOR KIDS

Regular white button mushroom have the most neutral flavour and are appealing to most kids. Omit the mustard.

NUTRITIONAL INFORMATION PER SERVING

Calories	441
Carbohydrates	6.0 g
Fibre	2.7 g
Protein	36.4 g
Fat	30.5 g
Saturated Fat	4.1 g
Cholesterol	100 mg
Sodium	232 mg

2 tsp (10 mL) vegetable oil
2 cups (500 mL) chopped mushrooms (button, oyster or cremini)
1½ tsp (7 mL) minced peeled garlic
Salt and pepper
½ cup (125 mL) sliced blanched almonds
2 Tbsp (30 mL) chopped fresh flat-leaf parsley leaves
1 Tbsp (15 mL) fresh lemon juice
1½ lb (750 g) tilapia or other white fish
1 Tbsp (15 mL) Dijon mustard

GARNISH

Chopped fresh flat-leaf parsley leaves
4 wedges lemon

1. Preheat the oven to 425°F (220°C). Line a baking sheet with foil lightly sprayed with vegetable oil.

2. In a large skillet over medium heat, heat the oil. Add the mushrooms, garlic, and salt and pepper and sauté for 5 to 8 minutes or until mushrooms are lightly browned and moisture has evaporated.

3. Transfer the mushroom mixture to the bowl of a food processor along with the almonds, parsley and lemon juice. Pulse just until well combined.

4. Place the fish on the prepared baking sheet and spread Dijon thinly over top of the fish. Divide the mushroom mixture among fish and pat down. Bake in the preheated oven for 10 minutes per inch of thickness or until the fish flakes easily with a fork (see page 112).

5. Serve garnished with parsley and lemon wedges.

WASABI MAYO SALMON SANDWICH

Cooked flaked salmon makes a wonderful sandwich (in fact, any leftover fish works well in this dish). Mirin is a type of rice wine similar to sake, but sweeter and with a lower alcohol content. If you don't have any mirin on hand, you can mix 1 tsp (5 mL) sugar with 3 Tbsp (45 mL) of white wine, vermouth or dry sherry, or substitute sake. Serve with Bok Choy and Mandarin Orange Salad with Ginger Dressing (page 34).

PREP TIME:
15
MINUTES

COOK TIME:
10
MINUTES

MAKES 4 SERVINGS

NUTRITION TIP

Wasabi, also known as Japanese horseradish, is a member of the Brassicaceae family, along with broccoli and cabbage, which contain a set of nutrients that help to promote liver health. Check the label to ensure the wasabi paste you are purchasing is real; many brands do not contain real wasabi, but rather combine horseradish with food colouring.

FOR KIDS

Omit the wasabi paste. You can make this sandwich using canned salmon or a milder white fish such as tilapia or turbot.

NUTRITIONAL INFORMATION PER SERVING	
Calories	545
Carbohydrates	54 g
Fibre	7.0 g
Protein	33 g
Fat	19.7 g
Saturated Fat	2.9 g
Cholesterol	76 mg
Sodium	799 mg

3 Tbsp (45 mL) mirin or sweet rice vinegar

1 Tbsp (15 mL) white miso paste

2 Tbsp (30 mL) brown sugar

2 tsp (10 mL) toasted sesame seeds (see Tip, page 35)

1 lb (500 g) salmon fillet (skinless), sliced crosswise into 4 pieces

¼ cup (60 mL) reduced-fat mayonnaise

¼ cup (60 mL) reduced-fat sour cream or plain 1% yogurt

2 tsp (10 mL) wasabi paste

2 tsp (10 mL) fresh lemon juice

4 baguette rolls (about 3 oz/90 g each), split in half

1 cup (250 mL) lightly packed baby spinach leaves

½ small ripe avocado, halved, pitted, peeled and thinly sliced

16 thin slices (coins) English cucumber (unpeeled)

1. Preheat the oven to 425°F (220°C). Line a baking sheet with foil and lightly spray with vegetable oil.

2. In a small bowl, whisk together the mirin, miso, sugar and sesame seeds.

3. Place the salmon on the prepared baking sheet and brush with half of the mirin mixture. Bake in the preheated oven for 10 minutes per inch of thickness or until the fish flakes easily with a fork (see page 112).

4. Transfer the cooked salmon to a bowl. Using a fork, flake the salmon. Add the remaining mirin sauce and gently fold to combine. Set aside.

5. In a small bowl, combine the mayonnaise, sour cream, wasabi and lemon juice. Spread over 4 baguette halves. Top with the spinach leaves, salmon mixture, avocado and cucumber slices. Sandwich with top of baguette. Serve.

APRICOT GINGER GLAZED SALMON

I'm always looking for new and creative ways to prepare salmon. One of my current favourites is this apricot ginger glaze—its sweet yet spicy flavour really suits this tender, flaky fish. Wild-caught Pacific salmon, which spend most of their lives in the open ocean and consequently contain very low levels of toxins, are a healthy, sustainable choice. Be careful not to overcook the fish: Salmon is always tastiest when slightly undercooked (see How to Cook Perfect Fish, below). Serve with sautéed snow peas or sugar snap peas.

PREP TIME:
10 MINUTES

COOK TIME:
10 MINUTES

MAKES 4 SERVINGS **DAIRY FREE**

NUTRITION TIP

Salmon is rich in heart-healthy, brain-boosting omega-3 fatty acids, which help to reduce bad (LDL) cholesterol.

FOR KIDS

Omit the Dijon mustard and hot sauce. The omega-3s in salmon support the healthy development of children's cognitive function and vision.

NUTRITIONAL INFORMATION PER SERVING

Calories	489
Carbohydrates	35 g
Fibre	7 g
Protein	40 g
Fat	23 g
Saturated Fat	4 g
Cholesterol	100 mg
Sodium	246 mg

4 salmon fillets (skin-on; 6 oz/175 g each)
2 tsp (10 mL) Dijon mustard

APRICOT GINGER GLAZE
½ cup (125 mL) apricot jam
1 tsp (5 mL) sesame oil
1 tsp (5 mL) reduced-sodium soy sauce
½ tsp (2 mL) chopped garlic
½ tsp (2 mL) chopped peeled fresh ginger
½ tsp (2 mL) Sriracha or your favourite hot sauce

GARNISH
3 Tbsp (45 mL) finely chopped unsalted pistachios
⅓ cup (80 mL) thinly sliced dried unsulphured apricots

1. Preheat the oven to 425°F (220°C). Line a baking sheet with foil and lightly spray with vegetable oil.

2. Place the salmon on the prepared baking sheet. Spread mustard evenly over top of the salmon.

3. **Make the glaze:** In a bowl, whisk together the jam, oil, soy sauce, garlic, ginger and hot sauce. Transfer half of the sauce to a small bowl and reserve. Brush the remaining half of the glaze over the salmon. Bake in the preheated oven at 425°F (220°C) for 10 minutes per inch of thickness or until the fish flakes easily with a fork (see How to Cook Perfect Fish, below).

4. Spread pistachios and apricots over top of the fillets. Serve with the remaining glaze.

HOW TO COOK PERFECT FISH

To determine how long to cook fish, a good rule of thumb is to measure the thickest part of the fillet and then cook at 425°F (220°C) for 10 minutes per inch. You will know the fish is ready when the flesh flakes easily with a fork or the internal temperature reaches 130°F (54°C).

PUMPKIN SEED AND LIME-CRUSTED WHITE FISH

For those that have nut allergies, seeds have come to the rescue. I keep large bags of seeds such as pumpkin and sunflower seeds in my freezer so I'm always prepared. You can even toast them before freezing so you save time. The lime zest and juice goes so well with the crushed seeds and a mild white fish. You can always use lemons if you don't have limes.

PREP TIME:
10
MINUTES

COOK TIME:
10
MINUTES

MAKES 4 SERVINGS  GLUTEN FREE

NUTRITION TIP

Pumpkin seeds are packed with fibre, vitamins and minerals. They contain mono-unsaturated fats that help to lower your bad cholesterol (LDL) and increase the good cholesterol (HDL). Just 1/3 cup (80 mL) supplies half your daily protein needs!

KIDS TIP

Most children will enjoy these seeds over a mild fish. You can eliminate the zest and garlic, if desired.

NUTRITION INFORMATION PER SERVING

Calories	358
Carbohydrates	6.6 g
Fiber	2.2 g
Protein	35.6 g
Fat	17 g
Saturated Fat	2.9 g
Cholesterol	141 mg
Sodium	212 mg

TOPPING

⅔ cup (160 mL) toasted pumpkin seeds
¼ cup (60 mL) Parmesan cheese (2 oz/160 g)
2 Tbsp (30 mL) olive oil
2 Tbsp (30 mL) lime juice
1 tsp (5 mL) lime zest
1 tsp (5 mL) minced garlic

1½ lb (750 g) basa, tilapia, halibut, or other white fish fillets

1. Preheat the oven to 400°F (200°C) and spray a 9-inch (23 cm) baking dish with vegetable oil.

2. **To make the topping:** Place the seeds, cheese, oil, lime juice, zest, and garlic in a small food processor and pulse just until combined.

3. Divide the topping overtop of the fish. Bake for 10 minutes per inch (2.5 cm) of thickness or just until cooked.

HOISIN SALMON WITH GINGER SLAW

Asian flavours are a classic match for salmon. In this dish, a simple hoisin glaze brushed on the tender fish is perfectly paired with a crunchy ginger-flavoured coleslaw. To make this dish even easier to pull together, use pre-chopped packaged coleslaw mix, which is readily available at most supermarkets. You can even find brands that contain Asian vegetables, including bok choy, snow peas and broccoli. If you've got a little more time, you can always julienne your own selection of fresh vegetables. Serve with seasoned couscous.

PREP TIME:
10
MINUTES

COOK TIME:
10
MINUTES

MAKES 4 SERVINGS **DAIRY FREE**

NUTRITION TIP

Sesame oil and sesame seeds have been shown to help lower blood pressure and levels of sodium in the blood.

FOR KIDS

If your kids aren't fans of cole-slaw, try serving the salmon over a bed of grated carrots instead.

NUTRITIONAL INFORMATION PER SERVING

Calories	363
Carbohydrates	13.9 g
Fibre	2.4 g
Protein	40.2 g
Fat	15.8 g
Saturated Fat	2.4 g
Cholesterol	108 mg
Sodium	351 mg

SLAW

¼ cup (60 mL) orange juice

1 Tbsp (15 mL) rice wine vinegar

4 tsp (20 mL) hoisin sauce

2 tsp (10 mL) sesame oil

2 tsp (10 mL) minced peeled fresh ginger

1 tsp (5 mL) liquid honey

1 ½ tsp (7 mL) Sriracha or your favourite hot sauce

¼ cup (60 mL) chopped fresh cilantro leaves

4 cups (1 L) pre-packaged coleslaw

SALMON

4 salmon fillets (skinless; 6 oz/175 g each)

2 Tbsp (30 mL) hoisin sauce

2 tsp (10 mL) toasted sesame seeds (see Tip, page 35)

1. Preheat the oven to 425°F (220°C).

2. **Make the coleslaw:** In a large bowl, whisk together the orange juice, vinegar, hoisin, sesame oil, ginger, honey, Sriracha and cilantro. Add the coleslaw and toss until well coated. Set aside.

3. **Make the salmon:** Place the salmon on a baking dish lightly sprayed with vegetable oil. Brush the hoisin sauce over top. Bake in the preheated oven for 10 minutes per inch of thickness, until the salmon flakes easily with fork (see page 112).

4. To serve, divide the prepared slaw among serving plates. Arrange a piece of salmon on top of each serving and sprinkle with sesame seeds.

SALMON TROUT WITH CUCUMBER SALSA

Many varieties of trout are readily available. I prefer either Rainbow or Salmon trout, which have a delicate and nutty flavour. Trout cooks quickly and is a favourite among those who don't like stronger-tasting fish, and goes particularly well with this flavourful cucumber salsa.

PREP TIME:
10
MINUTES

COOK TIME:
5
MINUTES

MAKES 4 SERVINGS  **GLUTEN FREE**

NUTRITION TIP

Rainbow trout are farmed primarily in freshwater ponds where they are more protected from contaminants and fed a fishmeal diet that has been fine-tuned to conserve resources. One 2.5-ounce (75 g) serving of rainbow trout provides 128 calories. Trout is an excellent source of protein and has heart-healthy omega-3 fatty acids.

FOR KIDS

Children usually enjoy trout due to its milder flavour and soft texture. Remove the skin from the fish. You can omit the red onions, if desired, and substitute a milder cheese such as shredded Havarti or mozzarella.

- 1½ cups (375 mL) diced English cucumber (unpeeled)
- ½ cup (125 mL) diced red bell pepper
- 2½ oz (75 g) crumbled light feta cheese
- ¼ cup (60 mL) diced red onion
- 2 tsp (10 mL) olive oil
- 1 tsp (5 mL) freshly grated lemon zest
- 1 Tbsp (15 mL) fresh lemon juice
- 1 tsp (5 mL) minced garlic
- Salt and pepper
- 2 Tbsp (30 mL) chopped fresh dill or flat-leaf parsley leaves
- 1 lb (500 g) rainbow trout fillet (skin-on)

1. In a bowl, combine the cucumber, red pepper, feta, onion, oil, lemon zest and juice, garlic, salt and pepper, and dill. Spread over a serving dish.

2. Heat a large skillet over high heat. Lightly spray with vegetable oil. Place the fish skin side down in the hot pan and cook for about 3 minutes, just until the skin is crispy. Turn over, reduce the heat to medium-high and cook just until the fish is opaque and flakes easily with a fork (see page 112).

3. Place the cooked fish skin side up on top of the cucumber salsa. Serve.

NUTRITIONAL INFORMATION PER SERVING

Calories	207
Carbohydrates	4.4 g
Fibre	1.2 g
Protein	24 g
Fat	9.9 g
Saturated Fat	3.2 g
Cholesterol	65 mg
Sodium	359 mg

SALMON WITH PEA PESTO

I discovered a great use for sweet green peas: pesto! Serve it alongside grilled salmon or another favourite protein. Salmon goes incredibly well with the flavour of peas.

MAKES 4 SERVINGS    GLUTEN FREE   VEGETARIAN

NUTRITION TIP

Peas are high in fibre and protein, and can slow down the rate at which sugars are digested, which means they can prevent or lower the risk of type 2 diabetes.

FOR KIDS

Kids will love the sweetness of pea pesto. You can serve it with either chicken or beef if they are not fans of salmon.

NUTRITIONAL INFORMATION PER SERVING

Calories	460
Carbohydrates	11 g
Fibre	3 g
Protein	41 g
Fat	27 g
Saturated Fat	7 g
Cholesterol	100 mg
Sodium	280 mg

1 ½ lb (750 g) salmon fillet (skin-on)

PEA PESTO
2 tsp (10 mL) vegetable oil
1 cup (250 mL) diced onion
1 ½ tsp (7 mL) minced garlic
2 cups (500 mL) frozen green peas
¼ cup (60 mL) 2% evaporated milk
3 Tbsp (45 mL) freshly grated Parmesan cheese
1 Tbsp (15 mL) olive oil
Salt and pepper
2 Tbsp chopped mint, for garnish

1. Preheat the oven to 425°F (220°C). Line a baking sheet with foil and lightly spray with vegetable oil. (Alternatively, you can grill the fish on a barbeque.)

2. Place the salmon on the prepared baking sheet and bake in the preheated oven for 10 minutes per inch of thickness (see page 112).

3. **Meanwhile, prepare pea pesto:** In a skillet, heat the oil. Add the onion and sauté for 3 minutes, just until softened. Add the garlic and peas and cook for another 3 minutes, until the garlic is fragrant and the peas are bright green.

4. Transfer the pea mixture to a food processor. Add the milk, Parmesan, oil, and salt and pepper and process until very smooth.

5. To serve, spread an even amount of pea pesto on each serving dish. Top with the cooked salmon and garnish with the mint.

POULTRY

CHICKEN AND TURKEY have officially overtaken beef as the most popular meat consumed in North America. It is a healthier option, less expensive and so versatile. Chicken or turkey breasts are quick cooking and low in fat and calories. I like to remove the skin, which contains most of the saturated fat. When you buy skinless, boneless chicken breasts, each piece is actually half of a full breast. Pounding the breasts with a meat mallet makes stuffing them easier, and the breasts cook more quickly. Legs and thighs have a rich and juicier flavor. Ground chicken and turkey are leaner than ground beef and make great burgers, meatloaves and meatballs.

Once you get poultry home from the grocery store, remove the wrapping but don't wash it, as bacteria can spray all over. Wrap the poultry loosely in foil, put it on a plate or small platter and place in the coldest part of the refrigerator for up to 48 hours. If freezing, place the poultry in a resealable freezer bag and freeze for up to 4 months.

It's best to thaw poultry either in the refrigerator , in a bowl of cold water, or in a microwave. Do not defrost at room temperature; harmful bacteria may develop. Never refreeze raw poultry after thawing.

There are so many delicious dishes to choose from in this chapter. For a great summer dish, try Baked Chicken Thighs with Homemade Barbeque Sauce and Pineapple (page 129). During the fall try my Turkey Chili with Butternut Squash (page 120).

TURKEY CHILI WITH BUTTERNUT SQUASH

Chili—with vegetables, lean protein and beans—is a complete, satisfying and nutritious one-pot meal. If desired, you can substitute an equal amount of sweet potatoes for the squash, and use any variety of beans. Serve over rice or a baked potato.

PREP TIME:
23
MINUTES

COOK TIME:
15
MINUTES

MAKES 6 SERVINGS **GLUTEN FREE**

NUTRITION TIP

Commercial tomato sauce and canned tomatoes contain excess sodium. Just ½ cup (125 mL) carries 400 to 550 milligrams of sodium. Healthier options include making your own favourite sauce or using low-sodium canned tomatoes.

FOR KIDS

Serve this dish over rice, pasta or a baked potato. Butternut squash contains vitamin C and beta-carotene, which improves your child's immune system.

NUTRITIONAL INFORMATION PER SERVING

Calories	326
Carbohydrates	25 g
Fibre	7.4 g
Protein	22 g
Fat	15 g
Saturated Fat	2 g
Cholesterol	65 mg
Sodium	533 mg

2 tsp (10 mL) vegetable oil
1 cup (250 mL) diced onion
2 tsp (10 mL) minced garlic
2 tsp (10 mL) chili powder
1 tsp (5 mL) ground cumin
1 small jalapeño, finely chopped (with or without seeds)
1 lb (500 g) ground turkey or chicken
2 ½ cups (625 mL) tomato sauce (store-bought or homemade)
½ cup (125 mL) reduced-sodium chicken stock
2 cups (500 mL) diced peeled butternut squash
1 can (19 oz/562 mL) red kidney beans, rinsed and drained

GARNISH

¼ cup (60 mL) chopped fresh cilantro leaves
½ cup (125 mL) shredded light sharp (old) cheddar cheese
¼ cup (60 mL) reduced-fat sour cream

1. In a large saucepan over medium-high heat, heat the oil. Add the onion and sauté for 3 minutes, until softened. Add the garlic, chili powder, cumin and jalapeño and sauté for 2 minutes, until fragrant. Stir in the ground turkey, breaking it up with the back of a wooden spoon, and sauté until no longer pink, about 3 minutes.

2. Stir in the tomato sauce, stock, squash and beans. Bring to a boil, cover and reduce the heat to medium. Simmer for 15 minutes or just until the squash is tender.

3. Ladle the chili into bowls and garnish with cilantro, cheese and sour cream.

ASIAN TURKEY BURGERS AND SLAW

Asian flavours go well with turkey. For ease, I use a pre-packaged coleslaw mix, which can be found in the produce section of most supermarkets, but you can make your own slaw by grating a selection of your favourite vegetables—try white, red or green cabbage, carrots and broccoli. This dish is quite satisfying without the bun, but it's also delicious served on a whole-grain roll with sliced tomato and an extra dollop of hoisin sauce.

PREP TIME:
15
MINUTES

COOK TIME:
10
MINUTES

MAKES 4 SERVINGS **DAIRY FREE**

NUTRITION TIP

Turkey is an excellent source of lean protein and contains the amino acid tryptophan, a building block of the brain compound serotonin, which induces better sleep and calmness. Plus 4 ounces (120 g) of ground turkey contains only 163 calories, 8 grams of fat and 2 grams of saturated fat. Compare that with the same amount of ground beef, which contains 250 calories, 17 grams of fat and 7 grams of saturated fat.

FOR KIDS

Turn this burger into mini sliders for kids. Turkey contains vitamin B12, important for a child's brain function. If they don't like a store-bought slaw, simply serve this with some grated carrots. Omit the Sriracha.

NUTRITIONAL INFORMATION PER SERVING

Calories	262
Carbohydrates	15.6 g
Fibre	2 g
Protein	24.1 g
Fat	11.7 g
Saturated Fat	2.6 g
Cholesterol	75 mg
Sodium	467 mg

TURKEY BURGERS

1 lb (500 g) ground turkey

¼ cup (60 mL) unseasoned panko or dry breadcrumbs

3 Tbsp (45 mL) hoisin sauce

1½ tsp (7 mL) minced peeled fresh ginger

1 tsp (5 mL) minced garlic

¼ cup (60 mL) finely diced onion

2 tsp (10 mL) reduced-sodium soy sauce

1 tsp (5 mL) Sriracha or your favourite hot sauce

1 tsp (5 mL) sesame oil

SLAW

2½ cups (625 mL) packed coleslaw (pre-packaged or homemade)

2 Tbsp (30 mL) chopped fresh cilantro leaves

1 Tbsp (15 mL) hoisin sauce

1 tsp (5 mL) sesame oil

1 tsp (5 mL) minced peeled fresh ginger

1 tsp (5 mL) Sriracha or your favourite hot sauce

1 tsp (5 mL) toasted sesame seeds (see Tip, page 35)

1. **Make the burgers:** In a bowl, combine the turkey, panko, 3 Tbsp (45 mL) hoisin, 1½ tsp (7 mL) ginger, garlic, onion, soy sauce, 1 tsp (5 mL) Sriracha and 1 tsp (5 mL) oil. Divide the mixture into 4 equal portions and, using your hands, form into 4 patties.

2. Preheat a grill or heat a skillet to medium-high. (If using a skillet, lightly spray with vegetable oil.) Cook burgers for about 5 minutes per side or until cooked through and temperature reaches 165°F (74°C) on a cooking thermometer.

3. **Make the slaw:** In a large bowl, toss together the coleslaw, cilantro, hoisin, oil, ginger, Sriracha, and sesame seeds.

4. To serve, divide the burgers among the serving plates. Top each serving with slaw.

MEDITERRANEAN CHICKEN WITH SPINACH, FETA AND OLIVES

In Mediterranean cuisine, spinach, feta cheese and olives are everyday ingredients. Together they make a delicious topping for lightly breaded and sautéed chicken. It's a quick and easy meal, and can be prepped early in the day to enjoy as a low-stress meal later. Serve with herbed couscous.

PREP TIME:
15
MINUTES

COOK TIME:
12
MINUTES

MAKES 4 SERVINGS

NUTRITION TIP

Look for light feta cheese. Regular feta contains 75 calories and 6 grams of fat per ounce, compared to light feta, which contains 58 calories and 4 grams of fat.

FOR KIDS

If your kids are not fans of feta, use mozzarella cheese instead. Omit the olives, if desired.

NUTRITIONAL INFORMATION PER SERVING

Calories	438
Carbohydrates	30.6 g
Fibre	4.4 g
Protein	45.1 g
Fat	14.7 g
Saturated Fat	3.3 g
Cholesterol	145 mg
Sodium	752 mg

1 egg
2 Tbsp (30 mL) 2% milk or water
1 cup (250 mL) seasoned dry breadcrumbs
2 Tbsp (30 mL) freshly grated Parmesan cheese
1½ lb (750 g) boneless, skinless chicken breast, pounded to ¼ inch (6 mm) thick
4 tsp (20 mL) vegetable oil, divided
1 cup (250 mL) diced onion

1 tsp (5 mL) minced garlic
½ tsp (2 mL) dried basil
16 small cherry or grape tomatoes
8 cups (2 L) lightly packed fresh chopped spinach
¼ cup (60 mL) sliced pitted black olives
1 oz (30 g) crumbled light feta cheese

1. Prepare a breading station: In a shallow bowl, whisk together the egg and milk. In another shallow bowl, combine the breadcrumbs and Parmesan.

2. Dredge both sides of the chicken in the egg mixture, then in the breadcrumb mixture, coating both sides. Set aside.

3. Heat 2 skillets over medium heat. Lightly spray the pans with vegetable oil and heat 2 tsp (10 mL) of the oil. Add the coated chicken pieces and sauté until cooked through and no longer pink inside, 5 to 8 minutes. Set aside.

4. Wipe out one of the skillets and place over medium heat. Heat the remaining 2 tsp (10 mL) oil. Add the onions, garlic and basil and sauté for about 3 minutes, until the onions are softened. Add the whole tomatoes and sauté just until the tomatoes begin to blister, 2 to 3 minutes. Add the spinach and sauté just until the spinach starts to wilt, about 2 minutes.

5. Divide the cooked chicken among the serving plates. Spread the spinach mixture over top of each serving. Sprinkle with the olives and feta. Serve immediately.

MOROCCAN CHICKEN WITH COUSCOUS

The whole family will love this delicious and comforting one-pot meal. The raisins complement the sweet and savoury flavours of this dish, and go well with the neutral flavour of the couscous. You can substitute chicken breast for the thigh if you prefer.

PREP TIME:
15
MINUTES

COOK TIME:
20
MINUTES

MAKES 4 SERVINGS **DAIRY FREE**

NUTRITION TIP

To eliminate one-third of the sodium from canned beans, rinse them under cold running water for at least 30 seconds before using. Just ½ cup (125 mL) of beans has close to 500 mg of sodium, which can be reduced to about 300 mg when rinsed.

FOR KIDS

Because kids often prefer less fatty meats, you may want to make this with chicken breasts instead of thighs. Substitute parsley for the cilantro, or omit the herbs entirely.

NUTRITIONAL INFORMATION PER SERVING

Calories	636
Carbohydrates	97.6 g
Fibre	6 g
Protein	36 g
Fat	12.5 g
Saturated Fat	2.5 g
Cholesterol	106 mg
Sodium	316 mg

1 cup (250 mL) couscous (preferably whole-wheat)
2 ½ cups (625 mL) reduced-sodium chicken stock, divided
1 lb (500 g) boneless, skinless chicken thighs or breasts, diced
3 Tbsp (45 mL) all-purpose flour
2 tsp (10 mL) vegetable oil
2 cups (500 mL) diced onion
1 cup (250 mL) diced carrot
2 tsp (10 mL) minced garlic
½ tsp (2 mL) ground cumin
½ tsp (2 mL) ground cinnamon
Salt and pepper
3 Tbsp (45 mL) tomato paste
1 cup (250 mL) golden raisins
1 can (15 ½ oz/459 mL) chickpeas, rinsed and drained
2 Tbsp (30 mL) fresh lemon juice
⅓ cup (80 mL) chopped fresh cilantro leaves, for garnish

1. In a saucepan, combine the couscous and 1 cup (250 mL) of the stock and bring to a boil. Cover and remove from the heat. Set aside for 5 minutes. Fluff with a fork.

2. Meanwhile, in a bowl or resealable bag, combine the chicken and flour and toss until the chicken is well coated.

3. Heat a large skillet over medium-high heat. Lightly spray the skillet with vegetable oil. Add the floured chicken and sauté for 3 minutes or just until lightly browned. Transfer the chicken to a plate.

4. In the same skillet over medium-high, heat the oil. Add the onion and sauté for 5 minutes, until softened. Add the carrot, garlic, cumin, cinnamon, and salt and pepper and sauté for 5 minutes. Return the chicken to the pan along with the remaining stock, tomato paste, raisins, chickpeas and lemon juice. Bring to a boil, cover and reduce the heat to low. Simmer for 8 minutes, just until the sauce is slightly thickened.

5. To serve, divide the cooked couscous among serving plates. Pour the chicken with sauce over the couscous and garnish with the cilantro.

PROSCIUTTO-WRAPPED CHICKEN BURGERS WITH SUN-DRIED TOMATOES

Chicken burgers—made with lean ground chicken, sun-dried tomatoes and Parmesan cheese—are taken to the next level by a thin layer of salty prosciutto. Top with a Sriracha mayo spread and arugula and you've got one unique and tasty burger. (This burger is also fantastic made with ground turkey.)

PREP TIME:
15
MINUTES

COOK TIME:
8
MINUTES

MAKES 4 SERVINGS

NUTRITION TIP

When selecting either lean ground chicken or turkey, remember that white meat has fewer calories and less fat than the dark meat. Dark meat can have close to three times the fat. Check the label or ask your butcher.

FOR KIDS

Omit the sun-dried tomatoes and Sriracha from the mayonnaise. You may also want to top the burger with a lettuce leaf rather than arugula, which some children find too bitter.

NUTRITIONAL INFORMATION PER SERVING

Calories	355
Protein	38.5 g
Carbohydrates	34 g
Fibre	6 g
Fat	17.2 g
Saturated Fat	7 g
Cholesterol	150 mg
Sodium	742 mg

1 lb (500 g) ground chicken or turkey
1 egg
¼ cup (60 mL) ketchup
⅓ cup (80 mL) unseasoned dry breadcrumbs
¼ cup (60 mL) rehydrated sun-dried tomatoes (see Tip, page 35)
¼ cup (60 mL) freshly grated Parmesan cheese
1 tsp (5 mL) minced garlic
Salt and pepper

4 slices thinly cut prosciutto (about 4 oz/120 g)
¼ cup (60 mL) reduced-fat mayonnaise
1 tsp (5 mL) Sriracha or your favourite hot sauce
4 hamburger buns
1 cup (250 mL) packed arugula or baby spinach leaves
4 slices tomato

1. In a bowl, combine the chicken, egg, ketchup, breadcrumbs, sun-dried tomatoes, Parmesan cheese, garlic, and salt and pepper. Using your hands, mix well. Divide the mixture into 4 equal portions and form into patties. Wrap each patty in one slice of prosciutto.

2. Preheat a grill or oven to 400°F (200°C) and cook for 8 to 10 minutes, just until the meat is no longer pink and the internal temperature reaches 165°F (74°C).

3. Meanwhile, in a bowl, combine the mayonnaise and Sriracha.

4. To serve, spread spicy mayo over the bottom half of the buns. Top each with the arugula, tomato and a burger and sandwich with the top of the bun.

LEMON CHICKEN SCALOPPINI

In this dish, slices of boneless chicken breast are pounded until thin, dredged in seasoned flour and then cooked in a flavourful sauce of lemon, honey and capers for an incredibly delicious result. Traditional scaloppinis are thickened with either butter or cream. Here, I use neither and simply allow the lemon stock base to thicken from the floured chicken. Serve with steamed jasmine rice.

MAKES 6 SERVINGS

PREP TIME:
10
MINUTES

COOK TIME:
14
MINUTES

NUTRITION TIP

Lemon is rich in vitamin C, which helps to keep our immune system strong, and is high in potassium, which helps to control blood pressure.

FOR KIDS

You can mellow the flavours of this dish for kids by adding an additional 2 tsp (10 mL) of honey and omitting the capers.

NUTRITIONAL INFORMATION PER SERVING

Calories	325
Carbohydrates	12 g
Fibre	0.6 g
Protein	37 g
Fat	9 g
Saturated Fat	1.6 g
Cholesterol	96 mg
Sodium	322 mg

Heaping ⅓ cup + 2 tsp (80 mL + 10 mL) all-purpose flour, divided

3 Tbsp (45 mL) freshly grated Parmesan cheese

Salt and pepper

1½ lb (750 g) boneless skinless chicken breast, pounded

2 tsp (10 mL) vegetable oil

⅓ cup (80 mL) dry white wine

¾ cup (185 mL) reduced-sodium chicken stock

2 tsp (10 mL) freshly grated lemon zest

2 Tbsp (30 mL) fresh lemon juice

1 Tbsp (15 mL) liquid honey

Salt and pepper

2 Tbsp (30 mL) capers (optional), drained

3 Tbsp (45 mL) chopped fresh flat-leaf parsley leaves

4 wedges lemon

1. In a shallow bowl, combine a heaping ⅓ cup (80 mL) of the flour, the Parmesan, and salt and pepper. Dredge the chicken in the mixture until both sides are well coated.

2. In a large skillet over medium-high heat, heat the oil. Add the coated chicken and sauté for about 2 minutes per side, just until lightly browned. Pour in the wine and cook just until evaporated, about 1 minute.

3. Meanwhile, in a bowl, whisk together the stock, lemon zest and juice, 2 tsp (10 mL) of the flour, honey, and salt and pepper. Add to the chicken, cover and simmer for 4 minutes, turning once, until the sauce is slightly thickened and the chicken is cooked through (should reach an internal temperature of 165°F/74°C when tested with a cooking thermometer).

4. To serve, divide the chicken among the serving plates, spooning the sauce over top. Garnish with capers (if using), parsley and lemon wedges.

BAKED CHICKEN THIGHS WITH HOMEMADE BARBEQUE SAUCE AND PINEAPPLE

Homemade barbeque sauce is so much tastier than commercial varieties. This sweet and savoury sauce goes perfectly with tender thighs and juicy pineapple, and is sure to appeal to the entire family. Serve over brown rice or with Pesto Mashed Potatoes on page 73.

PREP TIME:
10
MINUTES

COOK TIME:
19
MINUTES

MAKES 6 SERVINGS **DAIRY FREE**

NUTRITION TIP

One cup (250 mL) of chopped pineapple has only 74 calories and contains an entire day's worth of the recommended daily intake of vitamin C.

FOR KIDS

Often children prefer the taste and texture of canned pineapple to fresh, as it tends to be sweeter and softer. Pineapple contains bromelain, which is being tested for effectiveness in the prevention of asthma attacks.

NUTRITIONAL INFORMATION PER SERVING

Calories	395
Carbohydrates	41.5 g
Fibre	2.4 g
Protein	30.1 g
Fat	11.7 g
Saturated Fat	2.8 g
Cholesterol	141 mg
Sodium	179 mg

12 boneless, skinless chicken thighs
¼ cup (60 mL) all-purpose flour
2 tsp (10 mL) vegetable oil

BARBEQUE SAUCE
¼ cup (60 mL) apple cider vinegar
⅓ cup (80 mL) packed brown sugar
2 Tbsp (30 mL) blackstrap molasses
½ tsp (2 mL) Dijon mustard
½ tsp (2 mL) minced garlic
¼ cup (60 mL) ketchup
1 cup (250 mL) brown rice
2 cups (500 mL) reduced-sodium chicken stock

GARNISH
1 cup (250 mL) diced fresh or canned pineapple, drained
¼ cup (60 mL) diced green onions

1. Preheat the oven to 425°F (220°C).

2. In a bowl or resealable bag, combine the chicken and flour and toss until the chicken is well coated.

3. In a large skillet, heat the oil. Add the floured chicken and cook for 2 minutes per side, until browned on both sides. Transfer to a large baking dish.

4. **Make the barbeque sauce:** In a bowl, whisk together the vinegar, sugar, molasses, mustard, garlic and ketchup. Pour half over top of the browned chicken. Bake in the preheated oven for about 15 minutes or until the chicken reaches an internal temperature of 160°F (71°C) when tested with a cooking thermometer.

5. Meanwhile, in a saucepan, combine the rice and stock and bring to a boil. Cover, reduce the heat and simmer for 15 minutes or just until the rice is tender and the stock has been absorbed.

6. To serve, divide the cooked rice among the serving plates. Top each serving with an even amount of the baked chicken thighs. Garnish with pineapple and green onions and serve immediately, with the remaining sauce in a bowl for passing.

CHICKEN IN WILD MUSHROOM SAUCE

Creamy mushroom sauces are traditionally filled with calories and fat due to the butter and cream. To achieve the same effect with fewer calories, I use a combination of stock and evaporated milk; the addition of a bit of flour yields a creamy result. Use any variety of mushrooms you like, but be sure to cook them until all the liquid evaporates. Serve over steamed basmati rice.

PREP TIME:
10
MINUTES

COOK TIME:
16
MINUTES

MAKES 4 SERVINGS

NUTRITION TIP

Just ¼ cup (60 mL) of 2% evaporated milk has 100 calories and 2 grams of fat compared with the same amount of cream, which has over 200 calories and 22 grams of fat.

FOR KIDS

If your kids like mushrooms, stick with button mushrooms. Omit the Dijon. Don't worry about the wine since it evaporates during cooking.

NUTRITIONAL INFORMATION PER SERVING

Calories	370
Carbohydrates	16.1 g
Fibre	0.9 g
Protein	43.5 g
Fat	11.4 g
Saturated Fat	2.8 g
Cholesterol	101 mg
Sodium	350 mg

4 Tbsp (60 mL) all-purpose flour, divided

2 Tbsp (30 mL) freshly grated Parmesan cheese

Salt and pepper

1½ lb (750 g) boneless, skinless chicken breast, pounded

4 tsp (20 mL) vegetable oil, divided

3 cups (750 mL) sliced oyster mushrooms (about 8 oz/230 g)

2 tsp (10 mL) minced garlic

⅓ cup (80 mL) dry white wine

⅔ cup (160 mL) reduced-sodium chicken stock

⅔ cup (160 mL) 2% evaporated milk

1 tsp (5 mL) Dijon mustard

¼ cup (60 mL) chopped fresh flat-leaf parsley leaves, for garnish

1. In a shallow bowl, combine 3 Tbsp (45 mL) of the flour, the cheese, and salt and pepper. Dredge the chicken in the mixture until both sides are well coated.

2. In a large skillet, heat 2 tsp (10 mL) of the oil over medium-high heat. Add the coated chicken and sauté for 4 minutes, turning once, until lightly browned. Transfer to a plate and set aside.

3. In the same skillet, heat the remaining 2 tsp (10 mL) oil. Add the mushrooms and sauté for 5 minutes or just until lightly browned and no moisture is left. Add the garlic and sauté for 1 minute. Pour in the wine and sauté for 1 minute or until almost evaporated.

4. Meanwhile, in a bowl, whisk together the stock, milk, mustard and the remaining 1 Tbsp (15 mL) flour.

5. Stir into the mushroom mixture. Add the reserved chicken, cover, reduce the heat to low and simmer for 5 minutes, turning once, until the sauce is slightly thickened. (Do not increase the cooking temperature or the milk will curdle.)

6. To serve, divide the chicken among the serving plates, spooning the sauce over top. Garnish with the parsley.

CHICKEN WITH TOMATO, CHEDDAR AND SPINACH PESTO

This is a simple yet tasty chicken dish. When fresh basil is out of season, spinach pesto is a great alternative. I like to use the soft and tender baby spinach leaves, but large spinach leaves also work well as long as you trim any tough stems. In this pesto, almonds take the place of pine nuts, which are very expensive. Serve with steamed green beans.

MAKES 4 SERVINGS

NUTRITION TIP

Compared with beef, chicken is lower in fat and calories—4 ounces (120 g) of chicken breast contains 180 calories and 4 grams of fat; the same quantity of beef contains about 260 calories and 18 grams of fat.

FOR KIDS

As Popeye said, "Eat your spinach!" It's filled with vitamin K, which is good for growing bones. If your child prefers milder cheese, switch out the cheddar for mozzarella or Havarti.

NUTRITIONAL INFORMATION PER SERVING

Calories	420
Carbohydrates	10 g
Fibre	1.8 g
Protein	46.6 g
Fat	21.6 g
Saturated Fat	7.2 g
Cholesterol	117 mg
Sodium	490 mg

4 boneless skinless chicken breasts (6 oz/175 g each), pounded ¼ inch (6 mm) thick
3 Tbsp (45 mL) all-purpose flour
2 tsp (10 mL) vegetable oil
1 plum tomato, thinly sliced
1 cup (250 mL) shredded aged white cheddar cheese

SPINACH PESTO
1½ cups (375 mL) lightly packed spinach leaves
2 Tbsp (30 mL) olive oil
2 Tbsp (30 mL) reduced-fat mayonnaise
¼ cup (60 mL) freshly grated Parmesan cheese
3 Tbsp (45 mL) toasted sliced blanched almonds
1 tsp (5 mL) freshly grated lemon zest
1½ Tbsp (22 mL) fresh lemon juice
Salt and pepper

1. Preheat the oven to 350°F (175°C). Line a baking sheet with foil.

2. In a bowl or resealable bag, combine the chicken and flour and toss until the chicken is well coated.

3. In a large skillet over medium-high heat, heat the oil. Add the chicken and sear for about 1½ minutes per side (do not cook through).

4. Transfer the chicken to the prepared baking sheet and top each piece with an even amount of tomato and cheddar. Bake in the preheated oven for about 5 minutes, just until chicken is cooked through (should reach an internal temperature of 165°F/74°C when tested with a cooking thermometer) and cheese has melted.

5. **Meanwhile, prepare the spinach pesto:** In a small food processor, combine the spinach, olive oil, mayonnaise, Parmesan, almonds, lemon zest and juice, and salt and pepper and process until smooth (if the pesto is too thick, add a little water).

6. Place a dollop of pesto over top of each chicken breast, and serve.

CHICKEN WITH ROASTED CHERRY TOMATOES AND ASIAGO

Roasting cherry tomatoes brings out their natural sweetness; combining them with breadcrumbs and sharp cheese makes a delicious topping for baked chicken. (For a dairy-free entrée, omit the cheese.) If you'd like to make this dish even quicker to prepare, you can skip browning the chicken beforehand.

PREP TIME:
5
MINUTES

COOK TIME:
19
MINUTES

MAKES 4 SERVINGS

NUTRITION TIP

Chicken provides a significant portion of lean protein in your diet, which can help to ward off osteoporosis.

FOR KIDS

Substitute mozzarella or Havarti cheese for the asiago.

NUTRITIONAL INFORMATION PER SERVING

Calories	322
Carbohydrates	10.3 g
Fibre	1.5 g
Protein	39 g
Fat	12.7 g
Saturated Fat	4.2 g
Cholesterol	107 mg
Sodium	434 mg

1 ½ lb (750 g) pounded boneless, skinless chicken breast

2 cups (500 mL) red and yellow cherry or grape tomatoes, halved

1 Tbsp (15 mL) olive oil

1 tsp (5 mL) minced garlic

Salt and pepper

⅓ cup (80 mL) seasoned dry breadcrumbs

½ cup (125 mL) freshly grated Asiago cheese, for garnish

3 Tbsp (45 mL) chopped fresh basil leaves, for garnish

1. Preheat the oven to 350°F (175°C).

2. In a large skillet over medium-high heat, sear the chicken for about 2 minutes per side, until browned. Transfer to a baking dish.

3. In another baking dish, gently toss the tomatoes with the oil, garlic, and salt and pepper. Sprinkle with the breadcrumbs.

4. Transfer both baking dishes to the preheated oven. Bake the tomatoes for 15 minutes, until starting to brown and just blistered. Bake the chicken until it reaches an internal temperature of 165°F (74°C) or until no longer pink inside.

5. To serve, stir the tomato mixture to combine. Divide the chicken among the serving plates and top with the tomato mixture. Garnish with the cheese and basil.

THAI RED CURRY CHICKEN STIR-FRY

Stir-fries are a healthy way to get your protein, veggies and complex carbohydrates all in one easy dish. I love the Thai influence in this recipe—use a mild red curry paste, which is readily available in the Asian food section of supermarkets (we prefer Thai Kitchen brand). If you're going to serve this over noodles, choose a wider rice noodle.

PREP TIME:
15 MINUTES

COOK TIME:
12 MINUTES

MAKES 4 SERVINGS **DAIRY FREE**

NUTRITION TIP

Using light coconut milk versus the regular variety keeps this dish lower in fat and calories. Compared with ¼ cup (60 mL) of regular coconut milk, which contains 120 calories and 10 grams of fat, the same amount of light coconut milk contains only 45 calories and 4 grams of fat.

FOR KIDS

I would reduce the amount of curry paste by half, and use soy sauce rather than fish sauce, which will appeal to a child's taste buds.

NUTRITIONAL INFORMATION PER SERVING

Calories	273
Carbohydrates	7.8 g
Fibre	2.6 g
Protein	25.1 g
Fat	10.5 g
Saturated Fat	4.8 g
Cholesterol	62.6 mg
Sodium	633 mg

4 Tbsp (60 mL) all-purpose flour, divided

1 lb (500 g) boneless skinless chicken breasts or thighs, cut into 1-inch (2.5 cm) cubes

2 tsp (10 mL) vegetable oil

2 Tbsp (30 mL) red curry paste

1 Tbsp (15 mL) minced peeled fresh ginger

1½ tsp (7 mL) minced garlic

1 can (13.5 oz/400 mL) light coconut milk

1 tsp (5 mL) brown sugar

1 Tbsp (15 mL) fish sauce or reduced-sodium soy sauce

2 cups (500 mL) sliced red bell pepper

2 cups (500 mL) snow peas cut in half

3 Tbsp (45 mL) chopped fresh cilantro leaves

¼ cup (60 mL) chopped unsalted roasted cashews (optional)

3 cups (750 mL) cooked rice noodles (optional)

1. Place 3 Tbsp (45 mL) flour in a shallow bowl or resealable bag. Add the chicken and turn to coat well.

2. Heat a large skillet over medium-high heat. Lightly spray the pan with vegetable oil and sauté the coated chicken just until browned on both sides, about 3 minutes per side (do not cook through). Transfer the chicken to a plate.

3. Wipe out the skillet. Heat the oil over medium heat. Add the curry paste, ginger and garlic and sauté for 2 minutes, until fragrant. Stir the remaining flour into the coconut milk until smooth. Add to skillet and bring to a simmer. Add the sugar, fish sauce and browned chicken and simmer until the chicken is cooked through (should reach an internal temperature of 165°F/74°C when tested with a cooking thermometer) and sauce has thickened, about 3 minutes.

4. Meanwhile, heat a clean skillet over medium-high heat. Lightly spray with vegetable oil and sauté the red pepper and snow peas for 2 minutes, just until tender-crisp. Add to the chicken mixture. Sprinkle with cilantro and nuts (if using), and serve over top the rice noodles, if desired.

MEAT

SO MANY OF us love red meat, but as increased incidences of obesity, heart disease and cancer show, it does pay to limit our number of weekly servings to once or twice. Fortunately, choosing leaner cuts of meat, can help you keep your calories and fat in check. Try to limit your intake of higher fat cuts. Meat is a good source of protein, iron, zinc and B vitamins.

Most livestock is either grass-fed or grain-fed. Grass-fed cattle live on grassland for their entire lives. Meat from grass-fed cattle usually contains less total fat and calories than grain-fed meat. But grass-fed meat shines in the composition of fatty acids it contains: Grass-fed meat contains less saturated fat and more omega-3 fatty acids—as much as five times the amount—which makes it a leaner, healthier option than meat from corn-fed cattle.

Tightly wrapped fresh meat can be refrigerated for 2 days in the refrigerator. Fresh meat can be frozen for up to 6 months.

Defrost frozen meat in the refrigerator or in a bowl of cold water. You can also defrost it in the microwave according to direction.

For a taste of the Mediterranean, try Flank Steak with Tahini, Tomatoes and Feta (page 139). Or try my version of Bánh Mì (page 154)—it's authentic tasting and simple to make. For the kids, Beef Tacos with Cheddar cheese or the Mini Cheese and Prosciutto Meatloaves (page 149) will have them asking for seconds.

BEEF KOFTA WITH TAHINI SAUCE

A kofta is a Middle Eastern preparation for spiced ground meat shaped into a meatball or small meatloaf. Traditionally it is made with ground lamb or beef, but if desired you can use ground chicken to reduce the calories and fat. The addition of mint and cilantro, along with a dash of cinnamon, gives this dish its distinct flavour. To prepare the kofta, you roll the meat mixture into oval shapes, slide them onto skewers (optional) and then grill or bake them. Kofta goes well with homemade tahini sauce and diced vegetables. I love to serve it with warmed naan bread or a soft bun.

PREP TIME:
15
MINUTES

COOK TIME:
15
MINUTES

MAKES 4 SERVINGS

NUTRITION TIP

If you're watching your calories and fat, use either lean ground beef of ground chicken breast. Just 4 ounces (120 g) of ground lamb contains 320 calories and 26 grams of fat compared with ground chicken, which contains 160 calories and 8 grams of fat.

FOR KIDS

Make these with ground chicken, which has a milder flavour than beef, and omit the mint and cilantro. If your children don't like tahini sauce, you can serve these with ketchup.

NUTRITIONAL INFORMATION PER SERVING

Calories	377
Carbohydrates	11 g
Fibre	1 g
Protein	39 g
Fat	18 g
Saturated Fat	6 g
Cholesterol	189 mg
Sodium	384 mg

KOFTA

1 ½ lb (750 g) lean ground beef, lamb or chicken

½ cup (125 mL) minced onion

1 ½ tsp (7 mL) minced garlic

½ tsp (2 mL) ground cinnamon

2 eggs

½ cup (125 mL) unseasoned dry breadcrumbs

3 Tbsp (45 mL) chopped fresh mint leaves

¼ cup (60 mL) chopped fresh cilantro leaves

Salt and pepper

TAHINI SAUCE

2 Tbsp (30 mL) reduced-fat mayonnaise

2 Tbsp (30 mL) reduced-fat sour cream

2 tsp (10 mL) sesame oil

2 tsp (10 mL) reduced-sodium soy sauce

1 tsp (5 mL) tahini paste

GARNISH

½ cup (125 mL) diced seeded tomatoes

½ cup (125 mL) diced English cucumber (unpeeled) (optional)

Naan bread or soft roll (optional)

1. Preheat the oven to 400°F (200°C). Soak eight 6-inch (15 cm) wooden skewers in water or set aside 8 metal skewers (if using). Line a baking sheet with foil and lightly spray with vegetable oil.

2. In a large bowl, combine the ground beef, onion, garlic, cinnamon, eggs, breadcrumbs, mint, cilantro, and salt and pepper (use your hands to make sure all of the ingredients are evenly distributed).

3. Divide the mixture into 8 equal portions and form into oval shapes. If using skewers, slide 1 portion lengthwise onto each skewer.

RECIPE CONTINUED ON NEXT PAGE

BEEF KOFTA WITH TAHINI SAUCE CONTINUED

4. Heat a grill pan over medium-high heat. Working in batches, sear the koftas on each side for 2 minutes, until browned all over.

5. Transfer the browned kofta to a baking sheet. Bake in the preheated oven for 10 minutes or just until they reach an internal temperature of 160°F (71°C).

6. **Make the tahini sauce:** Meanwhile, in a bowl, whisk together the mayonnaise, sour cream, sesame oil, soy sauce and tahini paste. (If too thick, add a little water to reach the desired consistency.)

7. **Make the garnish:** In a bowl, combine the tomatoes and cucumber.

8. Serve koftas with the tahini sauce and garnish. If using naan bread, grill for 2 minutes per side, until lightly toasted, then cut into triangles and serve alongside koftas.

FLANK STEAK WITH TAHINI SAUCE, TOMATOES AND FETA

Grilled flank steak, flavourful tahini, diced tomatoes and crumbled feta transform this already healthy cut of beef into something wonderful. This is also delicious served at room temperature the next day. If desired, you can replace the flank steak with sirloin or New York strip.

PREP TIME:
15
MINUTES

COOK TIME:
15
MINUTES

MAKES 4 SERVINGS

NUTRITION TIP

Tahini is sesame seed paste. Sesame seeds are one of the best sources of calcium and are high in vitamin E and unsaturated fatty acids, which make them a heart-healthy addition. Sesame seeds can help remedy anemia.

FOR KIDS

If your child has never tried tahini sauce, serve a small amount on the side for them to dip their meat into. You can substitute shredded mozzarella or Havarti for the feta, if desired.

NUTRITIONAL INFORMATION PER SERVING

Calories	330
Carbohydrates	2.3 g
Fibre	0.5 g
Protein	38.1 g
Fat	17.7 g
Saturated Fat	6.6 g
Cholesterol	107 mg
Sodium	300 mg

1 ½ lb (750 g) beef flank steak

TAHINI SAUCE

2 Tbsp (30 mL) reduced-fat mayonnaise

2 Tbsp (30 mL) reduced-fat sour cream

1 Tbsp (15 mL) tahini paste

1 Tbsp (15 mL) water

2 tsp (10 mL) sesame oil

2 tsp (10 mL) reduced-sodium soy sauce

GARNISH

1 ½ oz (45 g) crumbled light feta cheese

⅓ cup (80 mL) diced seeded tomatoes

2 Tbsp (30 mL) chopped fresh cilantro or basil leaves

1. Preheat the oven to 400°F (200°C). Line a baking sheet with foil.

2. Heat a grill pan or skillet over medium-high heat. Lightly spray with vegetable oil and sear the steak for 2 minutes per side. Transfer the steak to the prepared baking sheet and bake in the preheated oven until it reaches desired doneness (about 10 minutes for medium rare or an internal temperature of 130 to 135°F/54 to 57°C).

3. **Make tahini sauce:** Meanwhile, in a small bowl, whisk together the mayonnaise, sour cream, tahini paste, water, oil and soy sauce.

4. To serve, slice the steak against the grain (crosswise) into thin slices. Arrange the slices on a platter and pour half of the sauce over top. Garnish with the feta, tomatoes and cilantro. Serve the remaining sauce on the side.

Pesto Smashed Potatoes (page 73), Flank Steak
with Caramelized Onions and Roasted Garlic.

FLANK STEAK WITH CARAMELIZED ONIONS AND ROASTED GARLIC

I'm always looking for tasty and interesting ways to serve flank steak. I find that if you just grill it, you tend to eat a larger portion, so here I caramelize a load of onions and whole garlic cloves to create a moist and delicious topping, which also counts as a vegetable. The key to caramelizing onions is to cook them over medium-low heat and stir often.

PREP TIME:
5
MINUTES

COOK TIME:
15
MINUTES

MAKES 4 SERVINGS **DAIRY FREE**  **GLUTEN FREE**

NUTRITION TIP

The phytochemicals in onions improve the working of vitamin C in the body, boosting the immune system. Onions also lower cholesterol and help to maintain a healthy blood pressure, which reduces the risk of heart disease and stroke.

FOR KIDS

Most children do not enjoy cooked onions and whole garlic. Instead, sauté finely diced vegetables that they do enjoy, such as bell peppers, carrots and mushrooms. The smaller the pieces, the better the chances they will enjoy it.

NUTRITIONAL INFORMATION PER SERVING

Calories	304
Carbohydrates	6.5 g
Fibre	0.7 g
Protein	35.7 g
Fat	14.1 g
Saturated Fat	5.1 g
Cholesterol	103 mg
Sodium	85 mg

2 tsp (10 mL) vegetable oil
2 lb (1 kg) large white onions, sliced into rounds (approx. 8 cups)
2 tsp (10 mL) Worcestershire sauce
2 tsp (10 mL) brown sugar
Cloves from 1 large head garlic, peeled
1½ lb (750 g) beef flank steak
Salt and pepper
3 Tbsp (45 mL) chopped fresh flat-leaf parsley leaves, for garnish

1. Preheat the oven to 425°F (220°C).

2. In a large skillet over medium heat, heat the oil. Add the onions and sauté for 5 minutes, just until softened. Stir in the Worcestershire, brown sugar and garlic cloves. Cover, reduce the heat to medium-low and cook for 15 minutes, stirring occasionally, until the garlic and onions begin to brown.

3. Season the steak with salt and pepper. Preheat a grill pan over high heat. Lightly spray the pan with vegetable oil. Sear the steak for about 5 minutes per side.

4. Transfer the seared steak to a baking sheet and cook in the preheated oven just until desired doneness (medium rare is about 130°F/54°C or about 10 minutes).

5. Let the steak rest for 5 minutes. Slice steak thinly and divide among serving plates. Top with caramelized onions and roasted garlic. Garnish with parsley. Serve.

BEEF STIR-FRY WITH BROCCOLI, SNOW PEAS AND EDAMAME

A trio of green veggies and an orange-flavoured sauce dress up this easy beef stir-fry. Use a good-quality lean steak and be careful not to overcook it. Serve this on its own or over a bed of noodles or brown rice.

PREP TIME:
15
MINUTES

COOK TIME:
10
MINUTES

MAKES 4 SERVINGS   **DAIRY FREE**

NUTRITION TIP

Strip loin steak is a leaner cut of beef and is quite good grilled or stir-fried. A 3-ounce (90 g) serving contains 140 calories and only 5 grams of fat, with 2 grams coming from saturated fat. Trim off all the visible fat from the edges before cooking.

FOR KIDS

Kids love the flavour of orange so this dish is sure to be a winner. To ensure your kids enjoy this dish, select only those vegetables they like and serve over a grain they prefer.

NUTRITIONAL INFORMATION PER SERVING

Calories	447
Carbohydrates	33 g
Fibre	8.1 g
Protein	33 g
Fat	19.3 g
Saturated Fat	4.4 g
Cholesterol	42 mg
Sodium	622 mg

SAUCE

¼ cup (60 mL) reduced-sodium soy sauce

¼ cup (60 mL) mirin or sweet rice wine vinegar or sake

¼ cup (60 mL) orange juice

2 tsp (10 mL) sesame oil

2 tsp (10 mL) liquid honey

1 tsp (5 mL) minced garlic

1 tsp (5 mL) minced peeled fresh ginger

2 tsp (10 mL) cornstarch

STIR-FRY

12 oz (340 g) strip loin steak

4 cups (1 L) chopped broccoli

2 tsp (10 mL) sesame oil

3 cups (750 mL) snow peas

2 cups (500 mL) frozen shelled edamame

GARNISH

⅓ cup (80 mL) chopped unsalted roasted cashews

2 tsp (10 mL) freshly grated orange zest

1. **Make the sauce:** In a bowl, whisk together the soy sauce, mirin, orange juice, sesame oil, honey, garlic, ginger and cornstarch until smooth.

2. **Make the stir-fry:** Heat a grill pan or skillet over medium-high heat. Sear steak for about 3 minutes per side, just until grill marks form. Transfer to a cutting board and slice thinly.

3. Using a steamer basket in a saucepan, steam the broccoli, just until bright green and still crisp, about 2 minutes. (Alternatively, you can place it in a microwave-safe bowl with a little bit of water, cover and cook on high for 3 minutes.)

4. In a large skillet or wok over medium heat, heat sesame oil. Add snow peas, edamame and steamed broccoli. Sauté for 2 minutes, until vegetables are tender-crisp. Stir in the prepared sauce and cook for 1 to 2 minutes, just until sauce is slightly thickened. Add the sliced beef and stir-fry just until the beef is heated through.

5. To serve, divide the stir-fry among serving plates and garnish with cashews and orange zest.

GREEK MEATBALLS OVER ORZO

Meatballs are always a hit with families. I've given a Mediterranean twist to these savoury meatballs and serve them over a bed of orzo, which is simply rice-shaped pasta. Add some diced tomatoes, olives, feta and mint and you have an upscale version of spaghetti and meatballs.

PREP TIME:
20
MINUTES

COOK TIME:
15
MINUTES

MAKES 4 SERVINGS

NUTRITION TIP

Ground lamb has more calories and fat than beef but is more flavourful. Four ounces (120 g) of lean ground beef has 234 calories and 17 g of fat, whereas ground lamb has 320 calories and 26 g of fat.

KIDS TIP

Finely chop the spinach, or omit completely, since many children don't like the green colour in their food. Remove the olives in the orzo as well.

NUTRITIONAL INFORMATION PER SERVING

Calories	490
Carbohydrate	43 g
Fibre	4 g
Protein	38 g
Fat	19 g
Saturated Fat	6 g
Cholesterol	115 mg
Sodium	720 mg

1 lb (500 g) lean ground beef or lamb
1 egg
¼ cup (60 mL) finely diced onion
⅔ cup (160 mL) crumbled feta cheese + 2 Tbsp (30 mL) for garnish, divided
½ 10 oz (300 g) box frozen chopped spinach, defrosted and drained
¼ cup (60 mL) seasoned breadcrumbs
½ cup (125 mL) chopped fresh mint or parsley
2 Tbsp (30 mL) barbeque sauce
½ tsp (2 mL) dried basil
¼ tsp (1 mL) dried oregano
2 tsp (10 mL) minced garlic, divided

ORZO
1 cup (250 mL) uncooked orzo
1 cup (250 mL) diced tomato
⅓ cup (80 mL) diced black olives
3 Tbsp (45 mL) lemon juice
2 Tbsp (30 mL) olive oil

1. Preheat oven to 425°F (220°C). Line a baking sheet with foil and spray with vegetable oil.

2. In bowl combine beef, egg, onion, ⅓ cup (80 mL) feta, spinach, breadcrumbs, ¼ cup (60 mL) mint, barbeque sauce, basil, oregano and 1 tsp (5 mL) garlic. Mix until combined and form into 12 meatballs. Place on baking sheet and bake for 15 minutes or until internal temperature reaches 160°F (71°C).

3. **Make the orzo:** Bring a pot of water to a boil and cook orzo for 8 minutes or just until tender to the bite. Drain and add tomatoes, olives, lemon juice, olive oil and remaining ⅓ cup (80 mL) feta, ¼ cup (60 mL) mint and 1 tsp (5 mL) garlic. Spoon orzo on serving plate, place meatballs over top. Garnish with remaining 2 Tbsp (30 mL) feta.

BEEF TACOS WITH CHEDDAR, TOMATO AND AVOCADO

Tacos are a perennial favourite. Making them yourself increases the flavour and nutrition. I like to use corn tortillas, which you can find in most well-stocked supermarkets. If you can't find them, use flour tortillas.

PREP TIME:

15

MINUTES

COOK TIME:

9

MINUTES

MAKES 6 SERVINGS

NUTRITION TIP

Corn tortillas contain much less fat, less sodium and more fibre than flour tortillas. Definitely the winner!

FOR KIDS

Kids will devour these. Let them make their own before heating.

NUTRITIONAL INFORMATION PER SERVING	
Calories	210
Carbohydrates	21.3 g
Fibre	3.3 g
Protein	13.2 g
Fat	8.6 g
Saturated Fat	2.7 g
Cholesterol	20 mg
Sodium	351 mg

2 tsp (10 mL) vegetable oil
¾ cup (185 mL) diced onion
1 tsp (5 mL) minced garlic
½ cup (125 mL) diced red bell pepper
2 tsp (10 mL) chopped seeded jalapeño
1 tsp (5 mL) chili powder
½ tsp (2 mL) ground cumin
6 oz (175 g) lean ground beef
⅓ cup (80 mL) medium salsa
⅓ cup (80 mL) canned black beans, rinsed and drained
6 small (6 inches/15 cm) corn or flour tortillas
½ cup (125 mL) shredded light cheddar cheese
⅓ cup (80 mL) diced seeded tomato
⅓ cup (80 mL) shredded romaine lettuce
¼ cup (60 mL) diced avocado

1. In a skillet over medium heat, heat the oil. Add the onion and garlic and sauté for about 3 minutes, until softened. Add the red pepper, jalapeño, chili powder and cumin and sauté for another 3 minutes, until the pepper is softened and spices are fragrant. Add the beef and cook until no longer pink, about 3 minutes. Stir in the salsa and beans and cook until heated through.

2. Warm the tortillas in a microwave on high for 20 seconds. (Alternatively, wrap them in foil and bake in a preheated 400°F/200°C oven for 5 minutes.)

3. To serve, place about ⅓ cup (80 mL) of the beef mixture in the middle of each tortilla. Top with the cheese, tomatoes, lettuce and avocado.

GREEK PHYLLO BURGER

I was thinking about how I could liven up a traditional burger and decided to try something unique. I wrapped it in phyllo pastry—turns out it's incredibly tasty! It reminds me a little of beef wellington, but without the fattening puff pastry. Feta cheese and tzatziki lend a Mediterranean taste to this winning burger.

PREP TIME:
15
MINUTES

COOK TIME:
22
MINUTES

MAKES 4 SERVINGS

NUTRITION TIP

About 1 oz (30 g/1 ½ sheets) of phyllo pastry contains only 85 calories and 1.6 grams of fat, compared with puff pastry, which contains 158 calories and 11 grams of fat.

FOR KIDS

If desired, substitute mild Havarti or mozzarella cheese for the feta. You can also omit the Dijon mustard. If your child doesn't like tzatziki, serve it with ketchup.

NUTRITIONAL INFORMATION PER SERVING

Calories	366
Carbohydrates	27.9 g
Fibre	1.6 g
Protein	27.9 g
Fat	14.8 g
Saturated Fat	5.8 g
Cholesterol	109 mg
Sodium	490 mg

½ cup (125 mL) finely chopped onion

1½ tsp (7 mL) minced garlic

½ tsp (2 mL) dried basil

1 lb (500 g) lean ground beef or lamb

1 egg

1 oz (30 g) crumbled light feta cheese

3 Tbsp (45 mL) unseasoned dry breadcrumbs

3 Tbsp (45 mL) barbeque sauce or ketchup

3 Tbsp (45 mL) chopped fresh cilantro or basil leaves

Salt and pepper

6 sheets phyllo pastry

4 tsp (20 mL) Dijon mustard

⅓ cup (80 mL) tzatziki (optional), for serving

1. Preheat the oven to 400°F (200°C). Lightly spray a baking sheet with vegetable oil.

2. Heat a skillet over medium heat and lightly spray with vegetable oil. Add the onions, garlic and basil and sauté for 5 minutes, just until the onions are softened and browned. Transfer to a bowl.

3. To the onion mixture, add the ground beef, egg, feta, breadcrumbs, barbeque sauce, cilantro, and salt and pepper and mix until well combined.

4. Divide the mixture into 4 equal portions. Using your hands, form into 4 patties.

5. Heat a skillet or grill pan over medium-high heat. Lightly spray with vegetable oil and sear the patties for about 1 minute per side, just until browned. Remove from the heat and set aside.

6. Layer the phyllo sheets on a clean work surface, lightly spraying every other sheet with vegetable oil. Using a sharp knife, cut into 4 squares.

7. Place one burger on top of each square. Brush mustard over the burger, then fold in the sides of the phyllo to make a neat parcel. Place each parcel seam-side down on the prepared baking sheet and bake in the preheated oven for 10 to 15 minutes, until they reach an internal temperature of 160°F (71°C). Serve with tzatziki (if using).

TORTILLA-WRAPPED SOUTHWEST BURGERS

For this recipe, I decided to do something a little different: I took a Southwestern-flavoured burger and wrapped it in a flour tortilla. No more bun! The fresh and tasty garnishes are served right on top of the tortilla. Moist, delicious and a show stopper.

MAKES 6 SERVINGS

NUTRITION TIP

Avocados are high in fat, but it's monounsaturated fat, which is a "good" fat that helps to lower bad (LDL) cholesterol. They do, however, contain a lot of calories. Just one avocado delivers 300 calories and 30 grams of fat. Use as a garnish.

FOR KIDS

Kids will love the appearance and taste of this unique burger. Add only the toppings they enjoy. If desired, you could replace the salsa with ketchup, and use a mild cheddar.

NUTRITIONAL INFORMATION PER SERVING

Calories	422
Carbohydrates	37 g
Fibre	7.3 g
Protein	28 g
Fat	9.7 g
Saturated Fat	7.3 g
Cholesterol	54 mg
Sodium	690 mg

1 lb (500 g) lean ground beef
1 tsp (5 mL) minced garlic
½ tsp (2 mL) ground cumin
½ tsp (2 mL) chili powder
¼ cup (60 mL) finely chopped green onion
3 Tbsp (45 mL) ketchup
1 egg
3 Tbsp (45 mL) unseasoned dry breadcrumbs
Salt and pepper

6 flour tortillas (8 or 10 inches/20 or 25 cm), preferably whole-wheat
1 cup (250 mL) medium salsa
2 cups (500 mL) shredded romaine lettuce
1 cup (250 mL) chopped plum tomatoes
1½ cups (375 mL) shredded light sharp (old) cheddar cheese
1 avocado, halved, pitted, peeled and diced

1. In a bowl, combine the beef, garlic, cumin, chili, onion, ketchup, egg, breadcrumbs, and salt and pepper. Using your hands, divide the mixture into 6 even portions and form into patties.

2. Heat a grill pan or skillet over medium-high heat. Lightly spray with vegetable oil and grill the patties for about 3 minutes per side, until cooked through.

3. Warm the tortillas in a microwave on high for 20 seconds. Divide the salsa over top the tortillas. Sprinkle with the lettuce, tomatoes, cheddar and avocado. Top each with a grilled burger.

4. To serve, fold in the 4 sides of the tortilla to enclose the burger. Place the burger seam-side down on a serving plate and slice in half. Repeat with the remaining burgers.

TORTILLA- AND CHEDDAR-CRUSTED MEATLOAF

Give new life to traditional meatloaf by infusing it with the flavours of the Southwest. Substituting finely ground tortilla chips for breadcrumbs, and salsa for ketchup, makes this a meatloaf you'll feel comfortable serving not just to family but also guests!

PREP TIME:
15
MINUTES

COOK TIME:
22
MINUTES

MAKES 4 SERVINGS

NUTRITION TIP

Compared with 12 traditional fried tortilla chips, which contain 16 grams of fat, 12 baked tortilla chips contain only 3 grams of fat!

FOR KIDS

Substitute mild cheddar or mozzarella cheese for the aged cheddar. You can also use barbeque sauce or ketchup instead of the salsa.

NUTRITIONAL INFORMATION PER SERVING

Calories	290
Carbohydrates	10.3 g
Fibre	0.6 g
Protein	28.7 g
Fat	14.7 g
Saturated Fat	6.4 g
Cholesterol	116 mg
Sodium	597 mg

1 lb (500 g) lean ground beef
1 tsp (5 mL) minced garlic
2 tsp (10 mL) Worcestershire sauce, divided
Salt and pepper
1 egg
1 cup (250 mL) baked corn tortilla chips (about 10), finely ground (about ¼ cup/60 mL)

¾ cup (185 mL) shredded light sharp (old) cheddar cheese, divided
⅓ cup (80 mL) + 1 Tbsp (15 mL) medium salsa
¼ cup (60 mL) ketchup

1. Preheat the oven to 400°F (200°C). Lightly spray an 8- × 4-inch (20 × 10 cm) loaf pan with vegetable oil.

2. In a bowl, combine the beef, garlic, 1 tsp (5 mL) Worcestershire, salt and pepper, egg, tortilla crumbs, ½ cup (125 mL) cheese and ⅓ cup (80 mL) salsa. Using your hands, mix until well combined. Pat into the prepared loaf pan.

3. In a small bowl, stir together the ketchup, 1 Tbsp (15 mL) salsa and the remaining 1 tsp (5 mL) Worcestershire. Spread over top of the meatloaf.

4. Bake in the preheated oven for 20 minutes or until it reaches an internal temperature of 160°F (71°C). Remove from the oven and sprinkle with the remaining ¼ cup (60 mL) cheese. Bake for 2 more minutes, until the cheese is melted.

5. Remove from the oven and let cool for 10 minutes before slicing.

MINI CHEESE AND PROSCIUTTO MEATLOAVES

If you're tired of Sunday night meatloaf, you have to try these simple and tasty muffin-cup meatloaves topped with crispy prosciutto and cheddar cheese. They cook in just a few minutes and make a nice appetizer or main dish. Be sure to use lean ground beef to reduce the calories and fat. Lean ground beef contains only 5% fat, whereas regular ground beef contains 20% fat—a big difference if you consume ground beef on a regular basis.

PREP TIME:
10
MINUTES

COOK TIME:
22
MINUTES

MAKES 6 SERVINGS

NUTRITION TIP

Serving portion-controlled meals is a great way to control your calories and fat. Two mini meatloaves contain 256 calories and 9 grams of fat. If you start your meal with a salad or soup, you can still enjoy a small dessert.

FOR KIDS

Kids love mini meals! If desired, omit the prosciutto and add some extra cheese.

NUTRITIONAL INFORMATION PER SERVING

Calories	256
Carbohydrates	14 g
Fibre	0.5 g
Protein	28 g
Fat	9 g
Saturated Fat	4 g
Cholesterol	118 mg
Sodium	553 mg

1½ lb (750 g) lean ground beef
2 eggs
½ cup (125 mL) barbeque sauce or ketchup
½ cup (125 mL) seasoned dry breadcrumbs
¼ cup (60 mL) finely sliced green onions
2 tsp (10 mL) minced garlic
1 tsp (5 mL) dried basil
Salt and pepper
1½ oz (45 g) finely chopped prosciutto
¼ cup (60 mL) shredded light cheddar cheese

1. Preheat the oven to 375°F (190°C). Lightly spray a 12-cup muffin pan with vegetable oil.

2. In a bowl, combine the ground beef, eggs, barbeque sauce, breadcrumbs, green onions, garlic, basil, and salt and pepper (use your hands to make sure all of the ingredients are evenly distributed). Divide evenly among the prepared muffin cups and lightly flatten with your fingers. Sprinkle each with the prosciutto. Bake in the preheated oven for about 20 minutes or just until they reach an internal temperature of 160°F (71°C).

3. Remove from the oven and sprinkle evenly with the cheese. Bake for another 2 minutes or just until the cheese has melted. Serve.

EGGPLANT MEATLOAF

Meatloaf is an all-time family favourite. If you want to take this ordinary Sunday night meal to new heights, try my updated recipe, which tops meatloaf with eggplant Parmesan—it's moist, delicious and healthy. You could use ground turkey or chicken instead of the ground beef.

PREP TIME:
10
MINUTES

COOK TIME:
20
MINUTES

MAKES 4 SERVINGS

NUTRITION TIP

Compared with 4 ounces (120 g) of regular ground beef, which contains 400 calories, 32 grams of fat and 12 grams of saturated fat, the same amount of lean ground beef contains only 200 calories, 8 grams of fat and 2.4 grams of saturated fat.

FOR KIDS

Try making this with zucchini if your children don't like eggplant. You can also make the meatloaf without the vegetable topping and just add the cheese.

MEATLOAF

1 lb (500 g) extra-lean ground beef
1 egg
⅓ cup (80 mL) barbeque sauce or ketchup
⅓ cup (80 mL) unseasoned dry breadcrumbs
¼ cup (60 mL) finely sliced green onions
1½ tsp (7 mL) minced garlic
½ tsp (2 mL) dried basil leaves
Salt and pepper
¾ cup (185 mL) tomato sauce (store-bought or homemade), divided

EGGPLANT

1 egg
2 Tbsp (30 mL) water or 2% milk
¾ cup (185 mL) unseasoned dry breadcrumbs
3 Tbsp (45 mL) chopped fresh flat-leaf parsley leaves
3 Tbsp (45 mL) freshly grated Parmesan cheese
8 eggplant rounds (¼ inch/6 mm thick) (unpeeled)
¾ cup (185 mL) shredded light mozzarella cheese

1. Preheat the oven to 400°F (200°C). Lightly spray a 9- × 9-inch (23 × 23 cm) baking pan with vegetable oil. Lightly spray a baking sheet with vegetable oil.

2. **Make the meatloaf:** In a bowl, combine the ground beef, egg, barbeque sauce, breadcrumbs, green onions, garlic, basil, and salt and pepper. Using your hands, pat it into the bottom of the prepared pan. Spread ½ cup (125 mL) of the tomato sauce over top. Set aside.

Calories	347
Carbohydrates	30 g
Fibre	2 g
Protein	34 g
Fat	10 g
Saturated Fat	5.2 g
Cholesterol	158 mg
Sodium	650 mg

3. **Make the eggplant:** In a shallow bowl, whisk together the egg and water. In another shallow bowl, combine the breadcrumbs, parsley and Parmesan, stirring well. Dip the eggplant in the egg mixture, then in the breadcrumb mixture, coating both sides. Place on the prepared baking sheet. Lightly spray the breaded eggplant with vegetable oil.

4. Transfer both the breaded eggplant and meatloaf to the pre-heated oven and bake for 15 to 20 minutes, until the meatloaf reaches an internal temperature of 160°F (71°C) and the eggplant is browned and tender. Remove the pans from the oven. Slice the eggplant pieces in half crosswise.

5. **Assemble the dish:** Arrange the baked eggplant slices in a single layer over top of the meatloaf. Spread the remaining ¼ cup (60 mL) tomato sauce over the eggplant. Sprinkle with the cheese. Bake for 5 minutes or until the cheese is melted. Remove from the oven and serve.

BUTTERNUT SQUASH SHEPHERD'S PIE

Nothing says comfort food better than a great-tasting shepherd's pie. Traditionally known as "cottage pie" in Britain, it was commonly made with leftover meat and topped with mashed potatoes. Here I put a healthy twist on the classic dish by topping it with mashed butternut squash combined with a hint of aged cheddar. I also add edamame (rather than the traditional green peas) to the ground beef filling. Incredible!

PREP TIME:
15
MINUTES

COOK TIME:
20
MINUTES

MAKES 8 SERVINGS

NUTRITION TIP

Butternut squash is loaded with fibre and antioxidants known as carotenoids, which help protect against heart disease.

FOR KIDS

Most kids love the sweet taste of squash, but if yours don't, you can substitute an equal quantity of sweet potato or regular white potatoes. If using regular potatoes, choose Yukon gold, which have a smooth, buttery flavour.

1½ lb (750 g) butternut or acorn squash, peeled and cubed

2 tsp (10 mL) vegetable oil

1½ cups (375 mL) finely diced onion

2 tsp (10 mL) minced garlic

¾ cup (185 mL) finely diced carrots

1 lb (500 g) extra-lean ground beef

1½ Tbsp (22 mL) all-purpose flour

1½ Tbsp (22 mL) tomato paste

⅓ cup (80 mL) reduced-sodium beef or chicken stock

¾ cup (185 mL) tomato sauce (store-bought or homemade)

½ tsp (2 mL) dried basil

Salt and pepper

¾ cup (185 mL) frozen edamame

2 Tbsp (30 mL) olive oil

3 Tbsp (45 mL) freshly grated Parmesan cheese

¾ cup (185 mL) shredded light sharp (old) white cheddar cheese

1. Preheat the oven to 425°F (220°C). Lightly coat a large baking sheet and an 8- × 8-inch (20 × 20 cm) baking dish with vegetable oil.

2. Place the squash onto the prepared baking sheet, lightly spray with vegetable oil and roast in the preheated oven for 15 to 20 minutes, just until tender.

3. Meanwhile, lightly spray a large nonstick skillet with vegetable oil. Add the oil and heat over medium-high heat. Add the onion and sauté for 3 minutes, until softened. Stir in the garlic and carrots and sauté for 3 minutes. Stir in the ground beef and sauté for 3 minutes or until no longer pink, breaking up any large pieces with a wooden spoon as it cooks.

Calories	260
Carbohydrates	15 g
Fibre	2.3 g
Protein	25.6 g
Fat	11 g
Saturated Fat	3.4 g
Cholesterol	40 mg
Sodium	223 mg

4. Stir in the flour and cook for 1 minute. Stir in the tomato paste, stock, tomato sauce, basil, and salt and pepper. Cover, reduce the heat to low and cook for about 3 minutes or until the sauce has thickened. Stir in the edamame and cook for 1 minute, just until heated through. Transfer to the prepared baking dish.

5. Transfer the baked squash to a bowl and mash (leave oven on). Add the olive oil, Parmesan, and salt and pepper and stir well. Spread over the prepared meat filling. Sprinkle with the cheddar cheese and bake in the hot oven for 5 minutes, until the cheese is melted and the topping is slightly browned. Serve.

BÁNH MÌ (VIETNAMESE SANDWICHES)

Bánh mì is a popular Vietnamese sandwich. I like to use a long baguette with a crunchy crust. The bread is hollowed out and filled with a light mayonnaise mixture, a carrot daikon slaw and tender pork tenderloin. If you can't find daikon, you can grate larger radishes. You can also replace the pork with roasted chicken or turkey.

PREP TIME:
20
MINUTES

COOK TIME:
15
MINUTES

MAKES 4 SERVINGS

NUTRITION TIP

Daikon is considered a superfood. It's incredibly low in calories with only 24 per 1 cup (250 mL). It contains large amounts of enzymes that aid in fat and starch digestion as well as high levels of vitamin C, phosphorus and potassium.

FOR KIDS

Just use grated carrots for the slaw and omit the cilantro. You can also use roasted chicken slices rather than the pork.

NUTRITIONAL INFORMATION PER SERVING

Calories	408
Carbohydrates	54 g
Fibre	2.9 g
Protein	29.3 g
Fat	9.1 g
Saturated Fat	2.0 g
Cholesterol	62 mg
Sodium	784 mg

¼ cup (60 mL) liquid honey
¼ cup (60 mL) rice wine vinegar
5 tsp (25 mL) reduced-sodium soy sauce or fish sauce
1 Tbsp (15 mL) sesame oil
3 tsp (15 mL) Sriracha or your favourite hot sauce, divided
1 lb (500 g) boneless pork tenderloin
¾ cup (185 mL) grated carrot
¾ cup (185 mL) grated daikon or radish
2 green onions, chopped
1 baguette (20 × 2 ½ inches/ 50 × 6 cm)
3 Tbsp (45 mL) plain 1% yogurt
3 Tbsp (45 mL) reduced-fat mayonnaise
½ English cucumber, sliced into ribbons (use a vegetable peeler)
¼ cup (60 mL) chopped fresh cilantro leaves

1. Preheat the oven to 400°F (200°C). Line a baking sheet with foil and lightly spray with vegetable oil.

2. In a bowl, combine the honey, vinegar, soy sauce, sesame oil and 2 tsp (10 mL) Sriracha.

3. Place the pork on the prepared baking sheet and cover with half of the honey mixture. Roast in the preheated oven for 15 to 20 minutes or until the pork reaches an internal temperature of 145°F (93°C). Remove from oven and set aside to rest.

4. **Make the slaw:** Meanwhile, in a bowl, combine the carrot, daikon and green onions with the remaining honey mixture.

5. **Assemble the sandwich:** Slice the baguette crosswise into 4 equal pieces, trimming the ends. Slice each piece in half (if desired hollow out the bread to reduce the calories). Heat in a microwave on high for 30 seconds, just until warmed.

6. In a small bowl, whisk together the yogurt, mayonnaise and remaining 1 tsp (5 mL) Sriracha. Spread over each of the baguette slices. Divide the cucumber strips among the bottom halves.

7. Cut the roasted pork crosswise into thin slices. Layer over the cucumber. Top with the slaw and cilantro. Sandwich with the remaining baguette slices. Serve.

PORK TENDERLOIN WITH MANGO AVOCADO SALSA

The bright flavours of fresh mango avocado salsa are a perfect pairing for roasted pork tenderloin. Since the avocado is marinated with lemon juice, you can make the salsa earlier in the day and refrigerate it until needed. Searing the pork before cooking it through ensures a tender, juicy cut of meat.

PREP TIME:
15
MINUTES

COOK TIME:
25
MINUTES

MAKES 4 SERVINGS **DAIRY FREE** **GLUTEN FREE**

NUTRITION TIP

Pork is a lean meat, containing less fat than a chicken breast. Due to improved agricultural practices, you can now enjoy it cooked medium (to an internal temperature of 145°F/63°C).

FOR KIDS

Children will love this sweet salsa. Try dicing the pork and mixing it into the mango avocado salsa.

NUTRITIONAL INFORMATION PER SERVING

Calories	250
Carbohydrates	7.7 g
Fibre	2.1 g
Protein	33 g
Fat	9.5 g
Saturated Fat	2.2 g
Cholesterol	89 mg
Sodium	145 mg

1 ½ lb (750 g) pork tenderloin
¾ cup (185 mL) finely diced mango
½ cup (125 mL) finely diced ripe avocado
¼ cup (60 mL) finely diced red bell pepper
3 Tbsp (45 mL) finely diced red onion
3 Tbsp (45 mL) chopped fresh cilantro leaves
2 tsp (10 mL) olive oil
1 tsp (5 mL) minced seeded jalapeño pepper
1 tsp (5 mL) fresh lemon juice
Salt

1. Preheat the oven to 400°F (200°C). Line a baking sheet with foil.

2. Heat a skillet or grill pan over high heat. Sear the pork for about 3 minutes per side. Transfer to the prepared baking sheet and bake in the preheated oven for about 15 minutes or until the internal temperature reaches 145°F (63°C) for medium doneness.

3. Meanwhile, in a bowl, combine the mango, avocado, bell pepper, onion, cilantro, oil, jalapeño, lemon juice and salt to taste.

4. To serve, slice the pork into thin medallions and divide among the serving plates. Spoon the salsa over top.

PISTACHIO-CRUSTED PORK TENDERLOIN

Prized for its tenderness, pork tenderloin's mild flavour pairs well with this Dijon and pistachio crust. Searing the meat first helps to retain the moisture of this very lean cut of meat. Leftovers are great for sandwiches or adding to a salad the next day.

PREP TIME:
10
MINUTES

COOK TIME:
15
MINUTES

MAKES 4 SERVINGS    **GLUTEN FREE**

NUTRITION TIP
Due to improved agricultural methods, pork can now safely be served at a medium doneness (around 135°F/57°C) rather than well done (165°F/74°C). It is much tastier when served slightly pink.

FOR KIDS
Omit the Dijon mustard, and if your child doesn't like pistachios, simply replace it with a nut they prefer—pecans, almonds and peanuts are all usually good substitutes.

NUTRITIONAL INFORMATION PER SERVING

Calories	249
Carbohydrates	5.4 g
Fibre	1.5 g
Protein	25.3 g
Fat	13.9 g
Saturated Fat	2.8 g
Cholesterol	63 mg
Sodium	195 mg

1 lb (500 g) pork tenderloin
1 Tbsp (15 mL) Dijon mustard
½ cup (125 mL) shelled unsalted pistachios
3 Tbsp (45 mL) freshly grated Parmesan cheese
1 Tbsp (15 mL) olive oil
½ tsp (2 mL) minced garlic

1. Preheat the oven to 400°F (200°C). Line a baking sheet with foil.

2. Heat a skillet over medium-high heat. Lightly spray skillet with vegetable oil and sear the tenderloin for about 2 minutes per side, just until browned all over.

3. Transfer the seared tenderloin to the prepared baking sheet. Rub the mustard all over the tenderloin.

4. In a small food processor, combine the pistachios, cheese, oil and garlic. Process until the mixture is finely ground and begins to come together. Pat on top and sides of browned tenderloin.

5. Bake for 10 to 15 minutes, until the pork reaches an internal temperature of 145°F (63°C).

6. Remove from the oven and let rest for 10 minutes. Slice into medallions and serve.

DESSERTS

I'M A VERY healthy eater, but not a day goes by that I don't indulge in a small portion of home-baked dessert. All of my desserts contain less fat than the traditional versions. I use less oil, relying instead on either reduced-fat sour cream or plain 1% yogurt for a moist texture, and mashed bananas or cooked dates for natural sweetness. For a simple garnish, sift icing sugar or unsweetened cocoa powder over top.

Different types of ovens and bakeware can affect baking times. To be on the safe side, check for doneness 5 to 10 minutes before the baking time is up. Stick a toothpick in several different parts of the cake, starting in the thickest part. If it comes out wet, continue baking. Brownies are the exception: their centre should be slightly wet when ready.

Most of the desserts in this chapter can be stored for about 3 days in an airtight container at room temperature. Cheesecakes and other dairy-rich desserts should be kept refrigerated. Cakes, cheesecakes, brownies, muffins and loaves can be frozen for up to 3 months if wrapped tightly in plastic wrap. Do not freeze cakes with fruit toppings; instead, add the fruit just before serving.

For a sure-fire showstopper, make Chocolate Mousse Cookie Cups (page 161). For a fun family dessert, Light Chocolate Fondue (page 163) can be served with a variety of fruit. Apple Crisp with Raisins and Toasted Almonds (page 175) is a winner any time of year. For a healthier treat for kids, try No-Bake Cranberry Nut Butter Oatmeal Squares (page 172).

CHOCOLATE MOUSSE COOKIE CUPS

For a real showstopper, try these chocolate chip cookies shaped into cups and filled with white or dark chocolate mousse. Because it doesn't contain heavy cream, the mousse is lighter and lower in fat than regular mousse. Have some fun with the filling: You can make both a white and dark chocolate mousse and swirl them together or, if you don't want to bother making mousse, you can fill these with frozen yogurt or light ice cream.

PREP TIME:
20
MINUTES

COOK TIME:
18
MINUTES

MAKES 12 SERVINGS **VEGETARIAN**

NUTRITION TIP

Traditional mousse is made with 35% whipping cream, which drastically increases the calories, fat, saturated fat and cholesterol. The egg whites and sugar create a lower calorie and 0 fat substitute.

FOR KIDS

Your kids will love helping you prepare these—just be sure they don't eat all the batter!

NUTRITIONAL INFORMATION PER SERVING

Calories	139
Carbohydrates	19.5 g
Fibre	0.6 g
Protein	2.2 g
Fat	6.3 g
Saturated Fat	1.8 g
Cholesterol	29 mg
Sodium	51.3 mg

COOKIE CUPS
⅓ cup (80 mL) granulated sugar
1 large egg
2½ Tbsp (37 mL) vegetable oil
1 tsp (5 mL) pure vanilla extract
½ tsp (2 mL) baking powder
Pinch of salt
¾ cup (185 mL) all-purpose flour
¼ cup (60 mL) miniature semi-sweet chocolate chips

CHOCOLATE MOUSSE
¼ cup (60 mL) semi-sweet chocolate chips or white chocolate chips
1½ tsp (7 mL) margarine or butter
3 Tbsp (45 mL) egg whites
⅛ tsp (0.5 mL) cream of tartar
3 Tbsp (45 mL) granulated sugar
1 egg yolk

Berries, for garnish (optional)

1. Preheat the oven to 350°F (175°C). Lightly spray a 12-cup mini muffin pan with vegetable oil.

2. In a mixing bowl, using an electric mixer, cream together the sugar, egg, oil and vanilla. Add the baking powder, salt and flour and mix until well incorporated (if the dough seems sticky, mix in a little more flour). Fold in the chocolate chips.

3. Using your fingers, place about 1 Tbsp (15 mL) of dough into each muffin cup, pressing down to cover the bottom and sides (wet fingers, if necessary).

4. Bake in the preheated oven for about 18 minutes or just until browned.

5. Remove the tray from the oven. Using either your fingers or the round end of a wooden spoon, make a ¾-inch (2 cm) indent into the middle of each cookie for the mousse filling. Transfer the cookies to a wire rack to cool.

RECIPE CONTINUED ON NEXT PAGE

CHOCOLATE MOUSSE COOKIE CUPS CONTINUED

6. **Make the mousse:** In a microwave-safe bowl, combine the chocolate and margarine and heat in a microwave on high for 30 seconds or just until chocolate is beginning to melt. (Alternatively, use a double boiler.) Whisk until smooth. Set aside to cool.

7. Meanwhile, in another bowl, using an electric mixer, beat the egg whites and cream of tartar until foamy. Gradually add the sugar and beat until stiff peaks form.

8. Add the egg yolk to the chocolate mixture and whisk until smooth. Fold in the stiff egg whites until well incorporated.

9. Fill the cookie cups with the mousse. Garnish with drizzled melted chocolate or berries. Serve, or chill for 20 minutes to firm mousse.

LIGHT CHOCOLATE FONDUE

This is not an oxymoron! You can definitely have your chocolate and eat it too, without worrying about excess calories, fat and cholesterol. My fondue recipe uses 2% evaporated milk rather than heavy cream. The liqueur is optional. If you prefer a mocha flavour, substitute an equal amount of strong brewed coffee for the liqueur. What you dip is up to you: your favourite fresh fruit, dried fruit and even mini marshmallows!

PREP TIME:
10
MINUTES

COOK TIME:
8
MINUTES

MAKES 8 SERVINGS  GLUTEN FREE  VEGETARIAN

NUTRITION TIP

The darker the chocolate the healthier the nutrients. The cocoa bean can be a disease-killing bullet. Stick to chocolate that contains at least 70% cocoa, which contains antioxidants. Studies have shown that eating 1 oz (30 g) of chocolate daily can reduce heart disease and stroke and lower blood pressure.

FOR KIDS

It's best to let the kids dip fresh fruit with the fondue. Berries and bananas are a popular choice.

8 oz (230 g) semi-sweet chocolate chips
½ cup (125 mL) 2% evaporated milk
1 cup (250 mL) icing sugar
2 Tbsp (30 mL) corn syrup
2 Tbsp (30 mL) chocolate-flavoured liqueur (optional)
4 cups (1 L) sliced fresh fruit (such as sliced bananas, strawberries or pineapple), for serving

1. In a small saucepan over low heat, whisk together the chocolate and evaporated milk for 3 minutes or just until the chocolate is completely melted.

2. Whisk in the sugar, corn syrup and liqueur (if using) and simmer for 5 minutes, whisking constantly, until sugar is completely incorporated.

3. Transfer to a serving bowl or fondue set. Serve with your favourite fruit for dipping.

NUTRITIONAL INFORMATION PER SERVING (½ CUP/125 ML FRUIT WITH ¼ CUP SAUCE)

Calories	255
Carbohydrates	46 g
Fibre	3 g
Protein	2.4 g
Fat	8.8 g
Saturated Fat	5.2 g
Cholesterol	1.2 mg
Sodium	28.6 mg

OATMEAL ALMOND LACE COOKIES

These cookies have a lacy texture, making them a perfect light treat for the end of a meal. They contain very little sugar yet are perfectly sweetened due to the sprinkling of chocolate chips. The batter is flaky so use your fingers to pat it down firmly on the baking sheet.

PREP TIME:

5

MINUTES

COOK TIME:

12

MINUTES

MAKES 14 SERVINGS  **VEGETARIAN**

NUTRITION TIP

I use a nominal amount of butter in this dessert to help hold the cookie together after baking, which is fine.

FOR KIDS

You can make 28 smaller cookies rather than 14 bigger ones, which may be a better size for younger children.

NUTRITIONAL INFORMATION PER SERVING (1 COOKIE)

Calories	99
Carbohydrates	8 g
Fibre	1.4 g
Protein	1.6 g
Fat	5 g
Saturated Fat	1.7 g
Cholesterol	8.5 mg
Sodium	2.2 mg

2 Tbsp (30 mL) softened unsalted butter

2 Tbsp (30 mL) vegetable oil

⅓ cup (80 mL) granulated sugar

2 Tbsp (30 mL) 2% milk

1 tsp (5 mL) pure vanilla extract

1 cup (250 mL) large-flake rolled oats

⅓ cup (80 mL) sliced blanched almonds

3 Tbsp (45 mL) all-purpose flour

¼ cup (60 mL) semi-sweet miniature chocolate chips

1. Preheat the oven to 375°F (190°C). Lightly spray a baking sheet with vegetable oil.

2. In a mixing bowl, using an electric mixer, cream together the butter, oil and sugar. Add the milk and vanilla and mix until combined. Add the oats, almonds and flour and mix until combined. Fold in the chocolate chips.

3. Drop the dough by spoonfuls (about 2 Tbsp/30 mL at a time) on the prepared baking sheet, spacing about 2 inches (5 cm) apart (the dough may crumble; just use your fingers to pack it down).

4. Bake in the preheated oven for 12 minutes or just until lightly browned and crisp. Let cool on the sheet until crispy. Cookies are best eaten within 2 days.

Oatmeal and Almond Lace Cookies, Oatmeal
Chocolate Chip Cookies (page 166), and
Chocolate Chewy Cookies

OATMEAL CHOCOLATE CHIP COOKIES

With rolled oats, tangy yogurt, sweet molasses and raisins, and a hint of chocolate, this cookie is sure to be gobbled up (and they'll never know it's healthy).

PREP TIME:
10
MINUTES

COOK TIME:
15
MINUTES

MAKES 16 SERVINGS  **VEGETARIAN**

NUTRITION TIP

Use blackstrap molasses—it is rich in iron and high in calcium and magnesium. It's also a preferred sweetener for diabetics.

FOR KIDS

You can increase the fibre by using a combination of ½ cup (125 mL) whole-wheat flour and ½ cup (125 mL) all-purpose flour, as well as by substituting 1 cup (250 mL) of raisins for the chocolate chips.

NUTRITIONAL INFORMATION PER SERVING	
Calories	115
Carbohydrates	17.5 g
Fibre	0.9 g
Protein	1.8 g
Fat	4.5 g
Saturated Fat	0.8 g
Cholesterol	0.3 mg
Sodium	54.6 mg

1 cup (250 mL) all-purpose flour
½ cup (125 mL) large-flake rolled oats
1 tsp (5 mL) ground cinnamon
½ tsp (2 mL) baking soda
¼ tsp (1 mL) ground cloves
¼ tsp (1 mL) salt
⅓ cup (80 mL) plain 1% yogurt

¼ cup (60 mL) vegetable oil
⅓ cup (80 mL) packed brown sugar
2 Tbsp (30 mL) blackstrap molasses
1 tsp (5 mL) pure vanilla extract
½ cup (125 mL) raisins or dried unsweetened cranberries
¼ cup (60 mL) semi-sweet chocolate chips

1. Preheat the oven to 350°F (175°C). Line a baking sheet with foil and lightly spray with vegetable oil.

2. In a bowl, combine the flour, oats, cinnamon, baking soda, cloves and salt.

3. In another bowl, combine the yogurt, oil, sugar, molasses, vanilla, raisins and chocolate chips. Add the wet ingredients to the dry ingredients and stir just until combined. Drop the dough by spoonfuls (about 2 Tbsp/30 mL at a time) onto the prepared baking sheet, spacing about 1 inch (2.5 cm) apart and flattening slightly.

4. Bake in the preheated oven for 15 minutes for softer cookies or 20 minutes for crisp. Remove from the oven and let cool on the sheet. Cookies are best eaten within 2 days.

FLOURLESS CHOCOLATE PECAN COOKIES

Once you taste these chewy chocolaty cookies, you won't believe they don't contain any oil or flour. In fact, they are so delicious that you'll want to keep a container of these on hand at all times. The mixture comes together with just the moisture of an egg and the delicate texture of icing sugar.

PREP TIME:
10
MINUTES

COOK TIME:
10
MINUTES

MAKES 14 SERVINGS  **GLUTEN FREE** **VEGETARIAN**

NUTRITION TIP

Both icing sugar and granulated sugar contain similar amounts of calories, carbohydrates and sugar, but 1 cup (250 mL) of granulated sugar equals 1 3/4 cups (435 mL) of icing sugar.

FOR KIDS

For an extra treat, melt 2 Tbsp (30 mL) of white chocolate with 1 tsp (5 mL) of vegetable oil and drizzle over the cookies. Set aside until the chocolate has hardened.

NUTRITIONAL INFORMATION PER SERVING

Calories	88
Carbohydrates	16 g
Fibre	1 g
Protein	1 g
Fat	3.4 g
Saturated Fat	0.8 g
Cholesterol	13 mg
Sodium	5 mg

1 egg
1 tsp (5 mL) pure vanilla extract
2 tsp (10 mL) water
1½ cups (375 mL) icing sugar, plus more for garnish
⅓ cup (80 mL) unsweetened cocoa powder
¼ cup (60 mL) semi-sweet chocolate chips
¼ cup (60 mL) chopped pecans

1. Preheat the oven to 350°F (175°C). Line a baking sheet with foil and lightly spray with vegetable oil.

2. In a bowl, whisk together the egg, vanilla and water.

3. In another bowl, combine the sugar, cocoa, chocolate chips and pecans. Add the dry ingredients to the wet ingredients and stir well to combine (the batter will be sticky).

4. Drop the dough by the tablespoon (15 mL) to make 14 cookies, spacing about 1 inch (2.5 cm) apart.

5. Bake in the preheated oven for 10 minutes, until crisp. Remove from the oven and let cool on the sheet. Dust with icing sugar just before serving. Cookies are best eaten within 2 days.

BANANA CHOCOLATE CUPCAKES WITH CREAM CHEESE FROSTING

Everyone loves the combination of banana and chocolate, so I thought a banana chocolate cupcake would hit the spot! These are a delicious and lighter alternative to a slice of chocolate cake. The marbling of the white and dark batters and the creamy icing create a stunning visual effect. The best bananas for this recipe are overly ripe. (I like to freeze leftover bananas so I always have a supply on hand.)

PREP TIME:
15 MINUTES

COOK TIME:
15 MINUTES

MAKES 12 SERVINGS  VEGETARIAN

NUTRITION TIP

An everyday cupcake contains 400 calories and 20 grams of fat (which is usually a saturated fat such as butter, lard or vegetable shortening). This version contains about half the calories and more than half the fat, so you can feel better about indulging.

FOR KIDS

Kids love baking. Let them help you make these cupcakes, and while you are at it you can explain why a cupcake like this is nutritionally better than store-bought processed versions.

NUTRITIONAL INFORMATION PER SERVING

Calories	225
Carbohydrates	35 g
Fibre	1.0 g
Protein	3.4 g
Fat	8.8 g
Saturated Fat	1.2 g
Cholesterol	34.7 mg
Sodium	185.1 mg

BANANA BATTER
3 Tbsp (45 mL) vegetable oil
½ cup (125 mL) granulated sugar
1 large egg
1 large ripe banana, mashed (about ½ cup/125 mL)
1 tsp (5 mL) pure vanilla extract
¾ cup (185 mL) all-purpose flour
1 tsp (5 mL) baking powder
½ tsp (2 mL) baking soda
¼ cup (60 mL) plain 1% yogurt

CHOCOLATE BATTER
3 Tbsp (45 mL) vegetable oil
½ cup (125 mL) granulated sugar
1 large egg
3 Tbsp (45 mL) unsweetened cocoa powder
½ cup (125 mL) all-purpose flour
½ tsp (2 mL) baking soda
½ tsp (2 mL) baking powder
⅓ cup (80 mL) plain 1% yogurt

ICING
⅔ cup (160 mL) icing sugar
¼ cup (60 mL) light cream cheese

1. Preheat the oven to 350°F (175°C). Lightly spray a 12-cup muffin pan with vegetable oil or line with paper liners.

2. **Make the banana batter:** In a mixing bowl, using an electric mixer, cream together the oil and sugar. Add the egg, banana and vanilla and mix until well combined.

3. In a small bowl, stir together the flour, baking powder and baking soda. Working in batches, add the flour mixture to the banana mixture, alternating with the yogurt and stirring until each addition is incorporated before adding another. Set aside.

RECIPE CONTINUED ON NEXT PAGE

BANANA CHOCOLATE CUPCAKES WITH CREAM CHEESE FROSTING CONTINUED

4. **Make the chocolate batter:** In a clean mixing bowl, using an electric mixer, cream together the oil, sugar and egg and mix until well combined.

5. In a small bowl, combine the cocoa, flour, baking soda and baking powder. Working in batches, add the cocoa mixture to the egg mixture, alternating with the yogurt and stirring until each addition is incorporated before adding another.

6. Divide the banana batter equally among the muffin cups. Top each cup with an even amount of the chocolate batter.

7. Bake in the preheated oven for 15 minutes or until a tester inserted in the centre comes out clean. Remove from the oven and let cool completely in the pan.

8. **Make the icing:** In a small food processor, combine the icing sugar and cream cheese and purée until smooth (if too thick, add a little water until the desired consistency is reached). Smooth about 1 Tbsp (15 mL) of the icing on top of each cupcake. Cupcakes will keep in an airtight container for up to 3 days.

DATE MOCHA BROWNIES

Everyone loves brownies. I decided to bump up the nutrients by adding cooked dates. Try asking your guests what the secret ingredient is—they will never guess. A tablespoon (15 mL) of instant coffee provides the mocha flavour, which cuts the sweetness. These brownies freeze well, and the recipe can easily be doubled (just use a 9- × 13-inch/23 × 33 cm baking pan instead).

PREP TIME:
10
MINUTES

COOK TIME:
20
MINUTES

MAKES 12 SERVINGS  **VEGETARIAN**

NUTRITION TIP

Dried dates are a great source of energy and make a perfect low-calorie and fat-free snack. Six dates contain only 120 calories. They are also a good source of dietary fibre.

FOR KIDS

Sneaking healthy cooked dates into brownies is the best way to serve dessert to your children (omit the coffee). Serve these as an afternoon snack to keep children's energy levels up.

NUTRITIONAL INFORMATION PER SERVING

Calories	168
Carbohydrates	33.1 g
Fibre	2.4 g
Protein	2.2 g
Fat	4.5 g
Saturated Fat	1.3 g
Cholesterol	13.6 mg
Sodium	89.6 mg

6 oz (175 g) dried pitted dates, chopped (about 1¼ cups/310 mL)

1 cup (250 mL) water

1 Tbsp (15 mL) instant coffee granules

⅓ cup (80 mL) semi-sweet chocolate chips

2 Tbsp (30 mL) vegetable oil

¾ cup (185 mL) granulated sugar

⅓ cup (80 mL) unsweetened cocoa powder

1 egg

⅔ cup (160 mL) all-purpose flour

¾ tsp (4 mL) baking powder

½ tsp (2 mL) baking soda

Icing sugar, for garnish

1. Preheat the oven to 350°F (175°C). Lightly spray an 8- × 8-inch (20 × 20 cm) baking pan with vegetable oil.

2. In a small saucepan over medium heat, combine the dates, water and coffee and bring to a boil. Cover, reduce the heat to low and simmer for 10 minutes, until most of the water has been absorbed. Add the chocolate and stir until melted.

3. Transfer the mixture to a blender or food processor (hold the lid down with a towel to prevent hot liquid from leaking) and purée until smooth.

4. In a large bowl, whisk together the oil, sugar, cocoa and egg. Add the date mixture and stir until well incorporated. Add the flour, baking powder and baking soda and stir just until incorporated.

5. Pour the batter into the prepared pan and bake for 20 to 25 minutes or just until a skewer inserted into the centre comes out dry. Remove from the oven and let cool in pan.

6. To serve, slice and sprinkle with icing sugar.

NO-BAKE CRANBERRY NUT BUTTER OATMEAL SQUARES

I love a granola oatmeal square recipe that I don't have to bake. The peanut butter can be swapped out for any other nut butter or even soy butter if nut allergies are a concern. You can also use any variety of puffed cereal you like, such as puffed quinoa.

PREP TIME:
10
MINUTES

COOK TIME:
3
MINUTES

MAKES 12 SERVINGS   **VEGETARIAN**

NUTRITION TIP

Oil contains more calories and fat than butter but virtually no saturated fat or cholesterol.

FOR KIDS

Kids will love this healthier version of puffed rice squares. Use any variety of nuts and unsweetened dried fruit they like.

NUTRITIONAL INFORMATION PER SERVING

Calories	70
Carbohydrates	17 g
Fibre	0.8 g
Protein	3.5 g
Fat	5.8 g
Saturated Fat	0.8 g
Cholesterol	0 mg
Sodium	40 mg

¼ cup (60 mL) liquid honey
¼ cup (60 mL) smooth peanut butter
2 Tbsp (30 mL) brown sugar
1 Tbsp (15 mL) pure maple syrup
1½ tsp (7 mL) vegetable oil
⅛ tsp (0.5 mL) ground cinnamon
½ tsp (2 mL) pure vanilla extract
1 cup (250 mL) large-flake rolled oats
1 cup (250 mL) puffed rice cereal
¼ cup (60 mL) chopped almonds, toasted
½ cup (125 mL) unsweetened dried cranberries

1. In a saucepan over medium heat, combine the honey, peanut butter, sugar, maple syrup, oil and cinnamon. Bring to a boil, then reduce the heat and simmer, stirring occasionally, for 3 minutes, until the sugar has completely dissolved. Stir in the vanilla.

2. Meanwhile, in large bowl, combine the oats, cereal, almonds and cranberries. Add the peanut butter mixture and stir until well combined.

3. Pat the mixture into an 8- × 8-inch (20 × 20 cm) baking pan lightly sprayed with vegetable oil. Cover and refrigerate for about 30 minutes, just until firm. Cut into 12 even squares. Squares will keep in an airtight container for up to 3 days.

MINI BROWNIES WITH CREAM CHEESE CENTRES

When it comes to dessert, I love "mini" everything. Baking in mini muffin pans delivers just enough sweetness and satisfaction, and portion control is built in. The surprise in these moist and chocolaty delights is a smooth cream cheese filling.

PREP TIME:
15
MINUTES

COOK TIME:
12
MINUTES

MAKES 36 SERVINGS  **VEGETARIAN**

NUTRITION TIP

Light cream cheese contains 25% less fat and calories than regular cream cheese. You can also substitute 5% ricotta cheese if you want to further reduce the calories and fat.

FOR KIDS

Let your kids help make these special desserts. They're a healthier option than store-bought mini treats.

NUTRITIONAL INFORMATION PER SERVING

Calories	58.7
Carbohydrates	10.7 g
Fibre	0.4 g
Protein	1.3 g
Fat	1.6 g
Saturated Fat	0.9 g
Cholesterol	13.4 mg
Sodium	34.2 mg

6 ½ oz (190 g) light cream cheese, softened, divided
¼ cup (60 mL) granulated sugar
2 Tbsp (30 mL) 2% milk
2 tsp (10 mL) pure vanilla extract, divided
2 Tbsp (30 mL) semi-sweet chocolate chips
2 Tbsp (30 mL) hot water

1 cup (250 mL) packed brown sugar
½ cup (125 mL) unsweetened cocoa powder
2 Tbsp (30 mL) all-purpose flour
2 large eggs
¼ cup (60 mL) reduced-fat sour cream
3 Tbsp (45 mL) corn syrup

1. Preheat the oven to 350°F (175°C). Lightly spray a 36-cup mini muffin pan with vegetable oil.

2. In the bowl of a small food processor, combine 4 oz (120 g) of the cream cheese and the granulated sugar, milk and 1 tsp (5 mL) of the vanilla. Purée until smooth. Set aside.

3. In a small bowl, combine the chocolate chips and water, and microwave on high for 25 seconds or just until the chocolate begins to melt. (Alternatively, use a double boiler.) Stir until smooth. Set aside.

4. In the bowl of a food processor, combine the brown sugar, cocoa powder, flour, remaining 2 ½ oz (75 g) cream cheese, eggs, sour cream, corn syrup and remaining 1 tsp (5 mL) vanilla. Purée until smooth. Add the melted chocolate and purée until smooth.

5. Using a teaspoon, divide half of the chocolate mixture among the prepared muffin cups. Divide the cream cheese mixture evenly on top. Top with the remaining chocolate mixture.

6. Bake in the preheated oven for 12 minutes, just until the brownies feel slightly firm to the touch. Remove from the oven. Let cool slightly in pan.

7. Using the tip of a butter knife, carefully remove brownies from the pan. Sprinkle with icing sugar, if desired. Serve warm or refrigerate.

APPLE CRISP WITH RAISINS AND TOASTED ALMONDS

A fruit crisp is always a healthier way to enjoy dessert. Use a firmer apple for baking. I like Granny Smith, Mutsu or Honeycrisp—all have a sweet tartness and hold their shape well when baked. Avoid Macintosh and Red or Golden Delicious which are too soft and break down when cooked. You can also substitute other fruit; pears and berries work well. Frozen fruit also works, but you must defrost it and drain the excess liquid before using. Serve warm with a scoop of frozen yogurt.

PREP TIME:
15
MINUTES

COOK TIME:
25
MINUTES

MAKES 12 SERVINGS   **DAIRY FREE**   **VEGETARIAN**

NUTRITION TIP

"An apple a day keeps the doctor away" has never been more true. Apples are known to reduce bad cholesterol, which reduces your risk of heart disease and stroke. They are also a great food for weight loss because they contain a lot of fibre, which fills you up.

FOR KIDS

Use your child's favourite fruits. You can omit the nuts if they are a concern, and if desired you can substitute dried unsweetened cranberries for the raisins. Serve this with a scoop of frozen yogurt alongside and your child will be in dessert heaven.

NUTRITIONAL INFORMATION PER SERVING

Calories	246
Carbohydrates	42.5 g
Fibre	2.6 g
Protein	2.8 g
Fat	8.2 g
Saturated Fat	0.6 g
Cholesterol	0 mg
Sodium	4.3 mg

6 medium baking apples, peeled, cored and cut into ¼-inch (6 mm) slices

⅓ cup (80 mL) granulated sugar

1 cup (250 mL) packed brown sugar, divided

⅓ cup (80 mL) raisins

2 Tbsp (30 mL) cornstarch

1½ tsp (7 mL) ground cinnamon, divided

2 Tbsp (30 mL) fresh lemon juice

TOPPING

¾ cup (185 mL) all-purpose flour

¾ cup (185 mL) large-flake rolled oats

⅓ cup (80 mL) chopped toasted almonds (see Tip, page 35)

⅓ cup (80 mL) vegetable oil

2 Tbsp (30 mL) water

1. Preheat the oven to 375°F (190°C). Lightly spray a 9- × 13-inch (23 × 33 cm) baking pan with vegetable oil.

2. In a bowl, combine the apples, granulated sugar, ⅓ cup (80 mL) brown sugar, raisins, cornstarch, 1 tsp (5 mL) cinnamon and lemon juice and toss until the apples are well coated. Spread evenly over the bottom of the prepared pan.

3. In another bowl, stir together the flour, ⅔ cup (160 mL) brown sugar, oats, almonds, oil, water and the remaining cinnamon (the mixture should be crumbly). Sprinkle evenly over the apples.

4. Bake in the center of the preheated oven for 25 to 30 minutes, until the topping is crisp and golden and the apples are tender.

RASPBERRY OATMEAL SQUARES

I've always enjoyed date squares, so I decided to create a similar dessert using frozen fruit. I experimented and discovered that raspberries work really well. The result tastes like a double-crusted crisp. The key is to defrost the berries and drain the excess liquid very well. If there is excess water the mixture will be too watery. Serve this with a scoop of frozen vanilla yogurt (you'll thank me)!

PREP TIME:
15
MINUTES

COOK TIME:
30
MINUTES

MAKES 12 SERVINGS **DAIRY FREE**  **VEGETARIAN**

NUTRITION TIP

Raspberries contain powerful antioxidants that help fight heart disease and cancers, plus 1 cup (250 mL) of raspberries contains only 60 calories and provides over 54% of your daily vitamin C. Because frozen berries are picked at the height of freshness and flash frozen, they can be even healthier for you than fresh. They are often less expensive, too.

FOR KIDS

You can omit the nuts or use a variety that you know your kids will like. If your kids aren't keen on raspberries, a mixture of strawberries and blueberries makes a great-tasting square, too.

NUTRITIONAL INFORMATION PER SERVING

Calories	254
Carbohydrates	41 g
Fibre	2.4 g
Protein	3.3 g
Fat	8.6 g
Saturated Fat	0.4 g
Cholesterol	0 mg
Sodium	5 mg

3 cups (750 mL) frozen raspberries, defrosted and well drained
½ cup (125 mL) granulated sugar
⅓ cup (80 mL) orange juice
2 Tbsp (30 mL) cornstarch
7 Tbsp (105 mL) water, divided
1⅓ cups (330 mL) large-flake rolled oats
1 cup (250 mL) all-purpose flour
¾ cup (185 mL) packed brown sugar
⅓ cup (80 mL) vegetable oil
⅓ cup (80 mL) chopped toasted pecans (see Tip, page 35)
½ tsp (2 mL) ground cinnamon

1. Preheat the oven to 350°F (175°C). Lightly spray an 8- × 8-inch (20 × 20 cm) baking pan with vegetable oil.

2. In a saucepan over medium heat, combine the berries, sugar and orange juice. Bring to a boil.

3. In a small bowl, whisk together the cornstarch and 4 Tbsp (60 mL) water. Stir into the berry mixture and simmer, stirring occasionally, until thickened, about 3 minutes.

4. In a large bowl, combine the oats, flour, sugar, oil, remaining water, pecans and cinnamon and stir just until crumbly.

5. Transfer half of the oat mixture into the prepared baking pan, using your fingers to press it into the bottom of the pan. Spoon the berry mixture over top and sprinkle evenly with the remaining crumb mixture.

6. Bake in the preheated oven for 30 minutes, until topping is lightly browned. Remove from the oven and let cool completely in pan. Cut into 12 even squares. Squares will keep in an airtight container for up to 3 days.

ALL-DAY BREAKFAST

WE'VE BEEN TOLD for years that breakfast is the most important meal of the day. But most of us don't have the time to cook and serve a nutritious and filling breakfast in the wee hours of the morning. So why not get out of our rigid schedules and serve up breakfast for dinner! Restaurants and fast food establishments are all joining in on this trend.

Millennials are most interested in breakfast for dinner options and want more spicy flavours and ethnic influences. So I decided to create some fantastic breakfast for dinner meals that will satisfy your family and friends. These meals would also make a great Sunday brunch. My favourites are Potato Asparagus Hash with Sunny Side-Up Eggs (page 179), the Egg and Chicken "Mc" Sandwich (page 187) and the Breakfast Pizza with Eggs and Sausage (page 188). The key to cooking perfect sunny side up eggs is starting with a hot pan and continue cooking the eggs on a medium low heat just until the whites are set but the yolk is still loose. Enjoy and get cracking!

POTATO ASPARAGUS HASH WITH SUNNY SIDE UP EGGS

Here a healthy version of potato hash has become a trendy one-dish breakfast or dinner meal. No longer are we adding corned beef or fatty sausages to this dish for leftovers. I have crusty potato chunks, asparagus and a couple of sunny side up eggs, loosely cooked of course, sitting over top. It's beautiful to look at and better to eat.

PREP TIME:
15 MINUTES

COOK TIME:
22 MINUTES

MAKES 4 SERVINGS   **DAIRY FREE**   **GLUTEN FREE**   **VEGETARIAN**

NUTRITION TIP

This breakfast for dinner dish is with loaded with healthy vegetables, no meat and the benefits of whole eggs, which are a great source of protein and keep you full longer. One egg has only 75 calories, 6 grams of protein and 5 grams of healthy fat.

FOR KIDS

Eggs contain omega-3 fatty acids, which are important for a child's brain development and cognitive memory. If mushrooms are not popular, just increase the amounts of other vegetables used.

NUTRITIONAL INFORMATION PER SERVING

Calories	338
Carbohydrates	47 g
Fibre	7.2 g
Protein	10 g
Fat	10.2 g
Saturated Fat	2 g
Cholesterol	186 mg
Sodium	326 mg

24 oz (680 g) baby potatoes
1 lb (500 g) asparagus, trimmed and cut into ½-inch (1 cm) pieces
4 tsp (20 mL) vegetable oil
2 cups (500 mL) diced onion
2 tsp (10 mL) minced garlic
6 oz (180 g) button mushrooms, diced
1 cup (250 mL) chopped roasted peppers, jarred or roasted in oven
Salt and pepper
¼ cup (50 mL) chopped dill or basil
4 large eggs

1. In pot of boiling water, cook potatoes just until fork tender, about 12 minutes. Do not overcook. Drain, rinse with cold water and dice. Set aside.

2. Meanwhile, cook asparagus in boiling water for 2 minutes, just until tender. Set aside.

3. In a large skillet, heat oil and sauté onion, garlic and mushrooms for 5 to 8 minutes until tender. Add diced potatoes and sauté another 10 minutes, just until potatoes are tender and lightly browned. Add cooked asparagus, roasted peppers, salt and pepper, and dill or basil. Place on serving platter.

4. Meanwhile in a small skillet sprayed with vegetable oil, crack eggs gently and cook about 5 minutes uncovered just until yolks are still loose. With a spatula, carefully place eggs over top.

PORTOBELLO SUNNY SIDE UP EGGS WITH PROSCIUTTO AND CHEESE

A great light breakfast meal for dinner is this stuffed baked Portobello. I like to clean the mushroom well with a wet paper towel and remove the dark inside gills with a spoon.

PREP TIME:
10
MINUTES

COOK TIME:
18
MINUTES

MAKES 4 SERVINGS    **GLUTEN FREE**

NUTRITION TIP

I prefer using prosciutto rather than bacon. One ounce (30 g) of prosciutto has only 57 calories and 3.4 grams of fat compared to bacon, which has 153 calories and 12 grams of fat per ounce.

FOR KIDS

If your children don't like the size of this mushroom, you might try using small bottom mushrooms. Dice the prosciutto and scramble the eggs to put over top.

NUTRITIONAL INFORMATION PER SERVING

Calories	135
Carbohydrates	6.0 g
Fibre	1.8 g
Protein	15.0 g
Fat	7.0 g
Saturated Fat	3.3 g
Cholesterol	250 mg
Sodium	330 mg

4 medium Portobello mushrooms (stems and gills removed)
2 oz (60 g) diced chopped prosciutto, about 4 thin slices
¼ cup (60 mL) grated cheddar cheese
4 eggs

1. Preheat oven to 425°F (220°C). Spray a baking sheet with vegetable spray. Spray the Portobellos with vegetable oil.

2. Place on baking sheet and bake for 15 minutes or just until just tender. Remove baking sheet and pour off excess liquid from mushrooms. Pat dry. Divide the prosciutto and cheese among the mushrooms and bake for another 3 minutes.

3. Meanwhile, in a large skillet sprayed with vegetable oil, crack 4 eggs gently into pan or into a 2-inch (5 cm) mold and cook on medium heat, just until whites are cooked and yolk is still runny, about 3 minutes. Gently slide eggs over top and serve immediately.

PROSCIUTTO AND PESTO EGG MUFFINS

These egg muffins are a great light dinner served with a side salad or soup. If I'm eating a later dinner, these are perfect and won't leave me going to bed on a full stomach. Purchase a ready-made pesto or make your own using either basil or parsley leaves (see page 33).

PREP TIME:
5
MINUTES

COOK TIME:
15
MINUTES

MAKES 6 SERVINGS

NUTRITION TIP

The latest studies show that eating an egg a day does not increase the risk of cardiovascular disease in healthy people. Most studies have found that dietary cholesterol has little, if any, impact on blood-cholesterol levels.

FOR KIDS

Kids will love helping to prepare these egg muffins and enjoy the flavour of the various foods. If they don't like prosciutto you can replace it with sliced deli turkey without nitrates.

NUTRITIONAL INFORMATION PER SERVING

Calories	127
Carbohydrates	4.5 g
Fibre	0.6 g
Protein	9.8 g
Fat	7.7 g
Saturated Fat	2.3 g
Cholesterol	195 mg
Sodium	292 mg

3 slices whole-wheat bread
2 Tbsp (30 mL) pesto sauce (store-bought or see recipe page 33)
2 oz (60 g) prosciutto
6 eggs

1. Preheat oven to 400°F (200°C). Spray a 6-cup muffin tin with vegetable spray.

2. Toast bread slices. Trim crusts and cut six 2-inch (5 cm) diameter circles out of the bread. Place in the bottom of the muffin tin. Spread pesto sauce over the bread.

3. Line muffins tins with prosciutto slices over the bread. Crack eggs into each muffin cup.

4. Bake for 15 to 18 minutes or just until whites are cooked and yolks are still loose.

POTATO LATKE WITH SUNNY SIDE UP EGGS AND SMOKED SALMON

Potato latkes don't have to be served only on the Jewish holiday of Hanukkah. A delicious root vegetable patty served with a sunny side up egg makes a great light dinner served alongside a large tossed salad. The key is to squeeze out all the moisture from the potato, and don't rinse or you will wash away the starch that is needed to hold the pancake together.

PREP TIME:
10
MINUTES

COOK TIME:
20
MINUTES

MAKES 6 SERVINGS

NUTRITION TIP
Fried latkes would require at least ¼ cup (60 mL) oil to cook. By baking them you are eliminating over 500 calories and 55 grams of fat!

FOR KIDS
Kids love potato pancakes and serving with a whole egg gives them more benefits in terms of nutrition.

NUTRITIONAL INFORMATION PER SERVING (2 PANCAKES + 1 EGG)

Calories	158
Carbohydrates	14.4 g
Fibre	1.2 g
Protein	9 g
Fat	5.0 g
Saturated Fat	1.5 g
Cholesterol	200 mg
Sodium	232 mg

4 cups (1 L) peeled grated baking potato (approximately two 12 oz/340 g potatoes)
¼ cup (60 mL) grated onion
4 tsp (20 mL) all-purpose flour
Salt and pepper
6 eggs
2 Tbsp (30 mL) plain Greek yogurt
2 oz (60 g) diced smoked salmon

1. Preheat oven to 400°F (200°C). Line a baking sheet with foil and spray with vegetable oil.

2. Squeeze out all moisture from grated potatoes and onions. Add potatoes and onions to a bowl along with flour, salt and pepper. Make 12 small potato pancakes on baking pan. Spray with vegetable oil and bake for 15 minutes, turning over after 10 minutes.

3. In 2 large skillets sprayed with vegetable oil, crack 6 whole eggs and cook sunny side up, just until whites are cooked and yolk is still slightly loose.

4. Divide yogurt over each potato cake, then add smoked salmon and carefully place an egg over each one.

WAFFLE SANDWICH WITH SMOKED SALMON, AVOCADO AND CHEESE

Waffles have become a trendy alternative to bread slices. Restaurants are using waffles for breakfast, lunch and dinner sandwiches. You can make your own as long as you have a waffle machine or buy the frozen variety. They are a great alternative to bread or bagels in this recipe.

PREP TIME:
15
MINUTES

COOK TIME:
8
MINUTES

MAKES 2 SERVINGS

NUTRITION TIP

If you want to boost your fibre, use half whole-wheat flour. A ½ cup (125 mL) all-purpose flour has 1.7 grams of fibre, compared to 8 grams of fibre for ½ cup (125 mL) of whole-wheat flour.

FOR KIDS

Use the light cream cheese instead of goat cheese and don't add the capers. You can also go in a different direction and used sliced roasted turkey instead of the salmon and cheddar cheese slices instead of the goat or cream cheese.

1 cup (250 mL) all-purpose flour
2 tsp (10 mL) granulated sugar
1½ tsp (7 mL) baking powder
Salt
1 cup (250 mL) 2% milk
1 Tbsp (15 mL) vegetable oil
1 egg
2 romaine lettuce leaves
4 thin slices tomato
8 thin cucumber rounds
2 oz (60 g) smoked salmon
¼ cup (60 mL) diced avocado
⅓ cup (80 mL) diced red onion
1 oz (30 g) crumbled softened goat cheese or light cream cheese
1½ Tbsp (22 mL) light mayonnaise
1½ tsp (7 mL) capers (optional)

1. Combine flour, sugar, baking powder and salt in a bowl.

2. In another bowl combine milk, oil and egg. Add to flour mixture just until blended.

3. Preheat a 4-inch (10 cm) waffle iron and lightly coat with cooking spray. Spoon ½ cup (125 mL) of the batter over the pan, covering it completely. Cook for 3 to 4 minutes or until steaming stops; repeat with remaining batter. Makes 4 waffles.

4. Divide lettuce leaves, tomato, cucumber, salmon, avocado and red onion over top of 2 of the waffles. Combine the goat cheese, mayonnaise and capers, if using. Divide goat cheese mixture over top salmon and vegetable filling. Top each with the 2 remaining waffles to make 2 sandwiches.

NUTRITIONAL INFORMATION PER SERVING (1 SANDWICH)

Calories	510
Protein	22.0 g
Carbohydrates	64.0 g
Fibre	3.0 g
Fat	18.0 g
Saturated Fat	5.0 g
Cholesterol	130 mg
Sodium	675 mg

MINIATURE MEDITERRANEAN QUICHES

Quiche traditionally is a higher fat food due to the fat laden crust, number of eggs, cream and excess cheese. These mini quiches are lighter and delicious since I have removed the crust and used a good amount of Mediterranean vegetables.

PREP TIME:
10 MINUTES

COOK TIME:
23 MINUTES

MAKES 6 SERVINGS  VEGETARIAN

NUTRITION TIP
Buy the egg whites in pre-packaged containers. Two tablespoons of liquid egg whites equals one egg white. The white of the egg only has 15 calories compared to the yolk, which has 60 calories.

FOR KIDS
If your kids don't like mushrooms, substitute another vegetable such as bell peppers. You can also omit the spinach and substitute the cheese for a milder variety. This makes a great snack or meal.

NUTRITIONAL INFORMATION PER SERVING

Calories	102
Carbohydrates	6.0 g
Fibre	1.0 g
Protein	7.4 g
Fat	5.5 g
Saturated Fat	1.7 g
Cholesterol	96 mg
Sodium	237 mg

2 tsp (10 mL) vegetable oil
1 cup (250 mL) diced onion
1 tsp (5 mL) minced garlic
1 cup (250 mL) diced button mushrooms
2 cups (500 mL) chopped fresh spinach (or ¼ cup/60 mL defrosted and squeezed dry frozen spinach)
½ tsp (2 mL) dried basil
3 eggs
2 egg whites
2 oz (60 g) crumbled feta cheese, divided
2 Tbsp (30 mL) all-purpose flour
Salt and pepper

1. Preheat oven to 375°F (190°C). Spray a 6-cup muffin tin with vegetable spray.

2. In a hot skillet, add oil, onions, garlic and mushrooms. Sauté for 8 minutes until onions are soft and mushrooms are no longer wet. Add spinach and basil; sauté until spinach has wilted.

3. Add sautéed vegetables to bowl along with eggs, egg whites, three-quarters of feta, flour, and salt and pepper. Pour into muffin tin and sprinkle with remaining feta. Bake for 15 to 18 minutes or until egg is just set.

ROSE'S EGG AND CHICKEN "MC"SANDWICH

Forget about McDonald's McMuffin. Here is my homemade version, which is tastier and a lot healthier. Kids will love this for breakfast or dinner. Easy to make and you can always use left-over chicken.

PREP TIME:
10
MINUTES

COOK TIME:
10
MINUTES

MAKES 4 SERVINGS

NUTRITION TIP
Since protein is key, my version has 22 grams compared to the 16 grams found in McDonald's version. There's also less fat and calories in my recipe.

FOR KIDS
You can omit the roasted bell pepper and substitute with either fresh tomatoes or sliced cucumber.

NUTRITIONAL INFORMATION PER SERVING

Calories	278
Carbohydrates	28.6 g
Fibre	4.8 g
Protein	21.9 g
Fat	9.3 g
Saturated Fat	3.4 g
Cholesterol	209 mg
Sodium	581 mg

4 oz (120 g) boneless chicken breast
4 whole-wheat English muffins, sliced in half
½ cup (125 mL) grated cheddar cheese
½ cup (125 mL) chopped roasted peppers, jarred or roasted in oven
4 eggs

1. In heated skillet sprayed with vegetable oil, cook chicken on medium heat about 4 minutes per side, just until cooked through. Let cool, then slice thinly.

2. Toast English muffins in oven at 450°F (230°C) or in a toaster oven. Divide cheese and roasted peppers over top and heat for another minute, just until cheese melts. Divide sliced chicken over top.

3. Meanwhile in large skillet sprayed with vegetable oil, cook eggs in a 2-inch/5 cm mold if desired) for about 4 minutes, just until whites are cooked and yolk is slightly runny.

4. Slip chicken and eggs carefully onto 4 cheese-filled muffin halves and top with remaining halves.

BREAKFAST PIZZA WITH EGGS AND SAUSAGE

A pizza breakfast for dinner is a great meal. I like to use either a thin crust whole-wheat pizza crust or a naan bread, which is an oven-baked flatbread found in Indian cuisine. But naan are much higher in sodium. The scrambled eggs, sausage and salsa make this a great Tex-Mex meal.

PREP TIME:
10
MINUTES

COOK TIME:
15
MINUTES

MAKES 6 SERVINGS

NUTRITION TIP

A 2-ounce (60 g) turkey sausage has 112 calories and 6 grams of fat compared to a beef sausage, which has 190 calories and 16 grams of fat!

FOR KIDS

Children enjoy making their own pizza varieties. Let them play with various toppings that they like.

NUTRITIONAL INFORMATION PER SERVING

Calories	388
Carbohydrates	38.9 g
Fibre	2.7 g
Protein	22.0 g
Fat	15.8 g
Saturated Fat	4.4 g
Cholesterol	172 mg
Sodium	650 mg

2 tsp (10 mL) vegetable oil
1 cup (250 mL) diced onion
½ cup (125 mL) diced green pepper
1 tsp (5 mL) crushed garlic
3 oz (90 g) crumbled
   turkey sausage
3 eggs
2 egg whites
2 Tbsp (30 mL) 2% milk
Salt and pepper
⅔ cup (160 mL) medium salsa
1 (12 inch/30 cm) pizza crust
   or 2 naan breads
½ cup (125 mL) grated
   cheddar cheese

1. Preheat oven to 425°F (220°C). Line a baking sheet with foil.

2. In a small skillet, add oil and sauté onion, green pepper and garlic for 5 minutes. Add sausage and cook just until no longer pink. Set aside.

3. In a small bowl, add eggs, egg whites, milk, salt and pepper. In another small skillet sprayed with vegetable oil, add egg mixture and scramble just until cooked.

4. Spread salsa over pizza crust, add scrambled eggs, top with cheese and bake on prepared sheet for 10 minutes or just until crust is browned and crisp.

ACKNOWLEDGMENTS

I'D LIKE TO offer my heartfelt thanks to the following people, who helped to bring this book to life:

Nick Rundall, publisher—for your continuous support of my work and for bringing *Rush Hour Meals* to the families of our country.

Jesse Marchand, associate publisher—for your excellent and essential work.

Tracy Bordian, editor—for making my book read as well as it does. You're a joy to work with.

Diane Robertson, designer—for making this book look incredible.

Natasha Tsakiris—for your great efforts in promoting my latest book.

Mike McColl, photographer—for capturing the beauty of each dish through photography and food styling. The days spent working together and listening to great music were so enjoyable.

Roxanna Roberts—for the nutritional analysis. You're a true professional to work with.

Lisa Perri, my assistant—for the energy and time you put into everything we do and keeping me on a tight schedule.

Dr. Harvey Skinner, dean of health at York University—for bringing me on as an adjunct professor and continually supporting my work, especially with respect to children's health.

Peter Higley, chief executive officer of the Pickle Barrel and Glow Fresh Grill, and my mentor over the years—for giving me ongoing opportunities to develop healthy recipes for the restaurants and always supporting my book endeavours.

Dang Idala and Lori Diza, my wonderful household assistants—for helping me with the daily work on the book.

INDEX